Cash-flow Appraisal for Property Investment

Also by W.D. Fraser

Principles of Property Investment and Pricing

Cash-flow Appraisal for Property Investment

W.D. Fraser

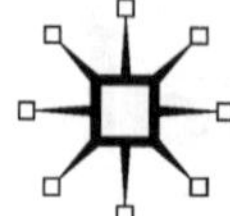

First published 2004 by
PALGRAVE MACMILLAN
Houndmills, Basingstoke, Hampshire RG21 6XS and
175 Fifth Avenue, New York, N.Y. 10010
Companies and representatives throughout the world

PALGRAVE MACMILLAN is the global academic imprint of the Palgrave Macmillan division of St. Martin's Press, LLC and of Palgrave Macmillan Ltd. Macmillan® is a registered trademark in the United States, United Kingdom and other countries. Palgrave is a registered trademark in the European Union and other countries.

ISBN 0–333–94641–3

This book is printed on paper suitable for recycling and made from fully managed and sustained forest sources.

A catalogue record for this book is available from the British Library.

10 9 8 7 6 5 4 3 2 1
13 12 11 10 09 08 07 06 05 04

Printed and bound in Great Britain by
Creative Print & Design (Wales), Ebbw Vale

Contents

List of Figures viii
List of Tables ix
Preface xi
Acknowledgements xiv

1 The Power of Compounding and Gearing 1
- Overview 1
- The miracle of compounding returns 3
- The impact of gearing 3
- Gearing in property investment 5
- Summary 8

2 The Time Value of Money: Compounding and Discounting 9
- Overview 9
- Traditional appraisal methods and their flaws 9
- The time value of money 12
- Compounding and discounting cash flows 16
- The concept of present value 18
- Periodic equivalent rates of return 19
- Summary 22
- Self-assessment questions 22
- Answers to self-assessment questions 23

3 Investment Decision-making by Discounted Cash Flow 27
- Overview 27
- The net present value 27
- The net terminal value 30
- The internal rate of return 32
- Summary 37
- Self-assessment questions 37
- Answers to self-assessment questions 39

4 Understanding the IRR and NPV 41
- Overview 41
- Understanding the IRR 41

	Multiple positive solutions (roots)	43
	Mutually exclusive projects	45
	The IRR method and risk	47
	Return on capital or cost of capital?	47
	Appraisal methods – summary of relative merits	48
	Summary	50
	Self-assessment questions	51
	Answers to self-assessment questions	53
5	**Key Principles for DCF Practice**	**59**
	Overview	59
	A perspective for DCF appraisal	59
	Capital rationing and project independence issues	60
	The relationship between cash flows and the required return	63
	Allowing for the cost of debt	64
	Sunk costs and opportunity costs	65
	The principle of incrementality	67
	Practical economics versus conventional accounting	68
	Summary	69
	Self-assessment questions	70
	Answers to self-assessment questions	72
6	**Estimating Cash Flows**	**77**
	Overview	77
	Dealing with inflation and growth	77
	Allowing for depreciation	79
	Allowing for taxation	80
	Capital allowances	81
	Application to practice	84
	Summary	93
	Self-assessment questions	93
	Answers to self-assessment questions	95
7	**Estimating the Required Return**	**101**
	Overview	101
	Components of the required return	102
	The required return of investing institutions	102
	The required return of corporate investors	104
	The direct cost of equity capital	104
	The direct cost of debt capital	107
	The concept of optimal financial gearing	108
	The weighted average cost of capital	110

	Adjusting the WACC for risk	111
	Application of the risk-adjusted WACC	112
	The CAPM and the cost of equity capital	114
	Using the CAPM to estimate a project's required return	117
	The adjusted present value method	120
	The CAPM approach: conclusion	124
	Summary	125
	Self-assessment questions	125
	Answers to self-assessment questions	127
8	**Short-cut DCF**	**131**
	Overview	131
	The relationship between return, growth, yield and rent review	131
	The market's implied growth expectation	136
	Depreciation through obsolescence	137
	Other applications	138
	Summary	140
	Self-assessment questions	140
	Answers to self-assessment questions	140
9	**Buy or Lease, and Leaseback Decisions**	**143**
	Overview	143
	The buy or lease decision	143
	The sale and leaseback decision	150
	Summary	154
	Self-assessment question	154
	Answer to self-assessment question	155
10	**Risk Analysis in Cash-flow Appraisal**	**157**
	Overview	157
	Risk in property appraisal	157
	Monte Carlo Simulation	161
	Sensitivity analysis	162
	Scenarios and the expected NPV	167
	Appraisal in equity analysis	169
	Summary	170
	Self-assessment questions	171
	Answers to self-assessment questions	172
Bibliography		173
Index		174

List of Figures

3.1	Relationship between NPV and IRR	34
7.1	Optimal gearing	109
7.2	Capital asset pricing model	116
10.1	Normal distributions: Investments A and B	160
10.2	Skewed distributions	161
10.3	Sensitivity analysis, Criterion Estates	166

List of Tables

1.1	The impact of gearing on growth	4
1.2	The impact of gearing on returns	6
1.3	The impact of gearing on risk	7
2.1	Projects A and B	10
2.2	Projects P and Q	22
3.1	Projects A and B	28
3.2	Project A – calculating the NPV	29
3.3	Project B – calculating the NPV	30
3.4	Project A – calculating the NTV	31
3.5	Project B – calculating the NTV	32
3.6	Project A, NPV at 12 per cent	35
3.7	Project A, NPV at 14 per cent	36
3.8	Project B, NPV at 20 per cent	36
3.9	Project B, NPV at 24 per cent	36
3.10	Projects P and Q	38
4.1	Project A	41
4.2	Project A, explaining the IRR	42
4.3	Projects C, D and E	44
4.4	Project E	45
4.5	Projects F and G	46
4.6	Incremental IRR method	47
4.7	Cash flows H and J	48
4.8	Estimating the IRR	51
4.9	Checking for multiple positive roots	52
4.10	Projects V and W	52
4.11	Projects X, Y and Z	53
4.12	Projects M and N	53
4.13	Project E, adjusted cash flow	57
4.14	Incremental IRR, Projects M and N	58
5.1	Projects A–F	60
5.2	Most profitable group of developments	62
5.3	Development projects J–O	70
5.4	Net cash flow per quarter, construction and sale	71
5.5	Development project	73
5.6	Expected cash flow, Western House	75

6.1	Project A: disaggregated cash flow	79
6.2	Plant and machinery allowances	82
6.3	The Birches Mall: current rentals	86
6.4	The Birches Mall: cash flow, Years 1–10	89
6.5	The Birches Mall: plant and machinery allowances	91
6.6	The Birches Mall: expected terminal value, Year 10	92
6.7	The Birches Mall: calculation of expected return	93
6.8	Toll Junction: P&M allowances	98
6.9	Toll Junction Industrial Estate: cash flows, Years 1–10	99
6.10	Toll Junction: expected net cash flow	100
7.1	Required premiums over gilt redemption yield	103
7.2	Alpha plc: cost of equity by rights issue	106
7.3	Alpha plc: cost of debt capital	108
7.4	Companies A and B	119
7.5	Example 7.5: Office investment	122
7.6	SAQ 7.5: Shopping centre	129
8.1	Example 8.1: expected cash flow	135
8.2	Example 8.3: expected cash flow	139
9.1	Value of taxation allowances, buy option	145
9.2	NPV of buy option	145
9.3	NPV of lease option	146
9.4	Incremental cash flows, buy and lease options	146
9.5	Repairs and insurance (after tax)	148
9.6	Estimated cash flows, Beans & Broccoli	149
9.7	Example 9.3: incremental cash flow	153
9.8	Incremental cash flow, SAQ 9.1	156
10.1	Sensitivity analysis, Criterion Estates	165
10.2	Scenario analysis, Orion Properties	169

Preface

The value of an investment can be considered as the value of the cash flow it is expected to generate in the future, discounted back to the present. That essential concept of discounted cash flow (DCF) applies universally to income-earning investments, and is fundamental to:

- understanding investment prices;
- the valuation of investments; and
- making investment decisions.

DCF is an integral part of modern financial theory, and DCF appraisal is the application of practical economics, adhering to logic and uncomplicated by irrational rules or conventions. DCF is a basis for the optimal selection of both portfolio investments (such as bonds, equities and standing property) and capital investment projects (including property development). It is consistent with the objective of maximising investors' wealth and, in the case of corporate investors, consistent with the objective of maximising shareholder value. In applying DCF to the appraisal of property investments, the analysis is undertaken alongside equities and bonds within mainstream financial theory, contrasting with traditional techniques which developed independently, resulting in different terminology, unnecessary mystique and confusion.

DCF techniques are particularly well suited to the appraisal of property investments because of the relative predictability of rental cash flows and a comparative lack of the interactions and inter-dependencies between investments or projects that can complicate appraisals in companies outside the property sector. Detailed appraisal may also be particularly rewarding to the property investor. The real estate market is notoriously opaque and imperfect, and perhaps relatively 'inefficient' in the pricing of investments. This may enable the astute investor to earn abnormal returns through rigorous appraisal, which would be impracticable in the more efficient context of the stock market. Whether real estate investments are priced efficiently or not, DCF is an essential aid to making rational investment decisions.

The principal aim of this book is to explain the application of DCF techniques to the appraisal of commercial real estate for the purpose of investment decision-making. This includes:

- decisions of investors (such as institutions, property companies or individuals) to buy or sell property investments;
- decisions of developers to redevelop or refurbish property; and
- decisions of business occupiers to buy or lease, or sell and leaseback a property.

Primarily, the book is intended as a practical guide to the application of DCF. But the scope for misuse of the technique is vast, through misunderstanding, confusion and error. Good practice requires an understanding of the underlying concepts and rationale as well as the principles, criteria and practical issues which inform the estimation of cash flows and choice of discount rate. The book has few academic pretensions, but it is important to draw on relevant financial theory in order to provide the reader with the extent and quality of understanding required to support good practice.

Learning a technique requires illustrations and practice. Hence, many examples are included to help the reader to assimilate the subject matter, and to bring clarity and insight to issues that may appear confusing in the text. Self-assessment questions are attached to each of the main chapters, and these the reader is recommended to work through. The text and examples draw primarily on UK experience, but their relevance is international.

It is important for a book about DCF practice to demonstrate how taxation may be incorporated into appraisals. This is included, but a detailed examination of taxation is beyond the scope of the book. Provision is made for stamp duty, corporation tax and capital allowances, but VAT is ignored, on the convenient assumption that, if it is payable then it is also recoverable. That is not always the case, and the reader requiring detailed information about taxation is advised to seek specialist advice.

Another issue that is highly relevant to DCF practice is the use of computers and specialist software. Computer spreadsheets such as Microsoft Excel are ideal for DCF appraisal, reducing dramatically the time and drudgery involved. But Excel is a formidable tool justifying a specialist text, and is beyond the scope of this book. Similarly, the book illustrates the application of DCF to property development decisions, but it is not a book about development appraisal or the development process. Incidentally, parts of the book are relevant to property valuation, but, again, it is not a book about valuation: it is about DCF appraisal for investment decision-making.

Primarily, the book is aimed at students on property management courses, at undergraduate or postgraduate levels, accredited by the Royal Institution of Chartered Surveyors (RICS). However, it will also be relevant to practising chartered surveyors, property consultants and others involved in the property business, including bankers involved in appraising appraisals. In the early chapters, no prior knowledge of the subject is required, and the process of compounding and discounting is covered from first principles. But as the analysis becomes more practical in later chapters, some basic knowledge of property investment is assumed, equivalent to the second or third year of an RICS-accredited undergraduate course.

W.D. Fraser

Acknowledgements

In preparing this book I have received help from a large number of people including Duncan Macaulay, Colin Cammidge of Drivers Jonas, Glen Watson of Wolfson & Co., and my colleagues at Paisley University, Ewan MacArthur, Stephen Edenborough and Norrie MacMillan. I would also like to thank DTZ Debenham Tie Leung for permission to include the data included in Table 7.1, Marlene Kilday for converting my barely legible scribblings into an immaculate typescript, and Becky Mashayekh of Palgrave Macmillan for her patience.

The book is the product of many years of teaching cash-flow appraisal to undergraduate and postgraduate students at Paisley University. My thanks are due to them for concentrating my mind and providing the inspiration for the book.

W.D. FRASER

1

The Power of Compounding and Gearing

OVERVIEW

Before addressing the techniques of cash-flow appraisal, the subject is introduced by raising the reader's awareness of the significance of compounding and gearing on investment performance over time. These concepts are fundamental to the subject of this book; in fact, fundamental to investment in general, including the business of pensions and life assurance.

THE MIRACLE OF COMPOUNDING RETURNS

Many authors have referred to the 'miracle' of compound interest; how wealth and the value of investments can be multiplied over time by the compounding of relatively modest annual returns. The concept is simple. If an investment worth £1,000 earns an annual return of 10%, and the £100 is reinvested along with the original capital at the end of the year, then a 10% return in the following year will provide a further £110 and a total value of £1,210 at the end of the second year. Provided the annual return continues to be 10% and is reinvested each year, then the investment will be worth £2,594 after ten years and £6,727 after twenty years.

The power of compounding is most impressive in the long term. In 1931, John Maynard Keynes (Keynes, 1931) predicted that the average standard of living in Britain would multiply by between four and eight times over the following hundred years. This attracted widespread scepticism at the time, particularly in view of the great economic depression of the inter-war period. Yet, in late 2003, the prediction is on track. Over the seventy years to the year 2000, the growth of real gross domestic product (GDP) per capita in the UK averaged almost 1.9% per annum, which translates into a growth multiple approaching four times. If that rate of economic growth is maintained until 2030, living standards will have multiplied by over six and a half times during the hundred-year period.

The power of compounding was illustrated more spectacularly by the performance of equity shares in the twentieth century. The recorded average return from UK equities of over 9.9% per annum (Barclays Capital, 2000) means that £100 invested in January 1900 could have been worth £1,285,872 at the end of the century (assuming dividend income was reinvested gross of tax). Even after adjusting for inflation, the real value of an equity portfolio could have multiplied 250 times over the century, an average real return of 5.7% per annum.

Over the post-1945 period of the twentieth century, £100 invested in UK equities would have grown to £103,120 in nominal (money) terms, and £4,520 in real terms (assuming income reinvested gross); annual returns averaging 13.7% and 7.3%, respectively. Over such long periods, it is important to allow for the impact of inflation by measuring returns in real terms. It is also important to appreciate the significance of reinvesting income to achieve the value growth noted above. If income is not reinvested, the value of a portfolio will merely compound at the capital gain element of total return. That would have reduced the growth of a notional £100 portfolio in 1945 to £8,396 at the end of the century – £368 in real terms.

Returns can be negative as well as positive (particularly after adjusting for the impact of inflation), and the effect of compounding negative returns over time can be as dramatic as the effect of positive returns. For much of the post-1945 period, UK government bonds (gilts) were ravaged by inflation. At the end of the twentieth century, £100 invested in irredeemable gilts in January 1946 would have been worth only £2 in real terms (£47 in nominal terms), assuming income was not reinvested. This represents an average real capital loss of nearly 7% per annum. Over the post-war period of the twentieth century, inflation wiped out 98% of the real value of undated government stock.

The examples above demonstrate how even modest annual rates of return can translate into dramatic changes in value over time. But the time periods considered have been long-term by comparison with the time horizon of most investment decisions, looking forward. Yet the power of compounding can still be highly significant over shorter periods. A compound annual return of 7.2% will double the nominal value of a portfolio in ten years, and 12.2% will multiply value ten times over twenty years (assuming income reinvested in each case). Such returns are broadly consistent with the performance of UK equities, gilts and property over the 1980s and 1990s. It is this ability of compounding returns to generate substantial wealth over time from modest savings that life assurance and pension schemes seek to exploit for the benefit of policy-holders and pensioners.

Like equity shares, property provides the investor with the opportunity to benefit from the innovations and productivity improvements that drive a country's economic growth. The value of housing in Britain in the early twenty-first century has grown to levels scarcely imaginable even in the 1980s, and commercial property provided double-digit average returns (nominal) through the 1970s, 1980s and 1990s. However, during most of the 1980s and 1990s, equity shares outperformed property. In fact, over the 1990s, the value of a typical portfolio of equities would nearly have quadrupled in value (if dividends were reinvested), whereas a typical property portfolio would 'merely' have doubled. This relatively sluggish performance of property drove several institutional investors to liquidate their property portfolios in favour of equities and bonds. But the value of property continued to grow in the first three years of the twenty-first century, while equity shares collapsed. Over that three-year period, returns from commercial property totalled nearly 30% (IPD, 2003), while the value of equities halved. That dramatic turnaround nicely highlights the importance of the relative performance of different asset classes and the timing of investment decisions.

THE IMPACT OF GEARING

Gearing (or leverage) is another important concept in understanding investment performance. Whatever is the underlying growth rate of an income stream over time, gearing provides the potential for enhancement. Take the case of an income of £100 per annum growing at a steady rate of 10% per annum, from which a fixed sum of £20 per annum is deducted (see Example 1 in Table 1.1). The growth rate of the residual income averages 11.6% per annum over the ten years. If the fixed deduction is raised to £50, the growth rate of the residual is increased to an average of 15.4% per annum (see Example 2). If the fixed deduction is £80, the growth rate of the residual income averages 24.5% per annum (Example 3).

The higher the income gearing ratio (the fixed deduction as a percentage of the basic income), the higher the growth potential of the residual income. In fact, the enhanced growth rate of the residual is proportional to the gearing ratio. The 50% gearing at Year 0 in Example 2 results in the Year 1 growth rate of the residual income being 20%, double the growth rate of the basic income. But as the basic income grows, the gearing ratio falls in each successive year, so the growth rate of the residual income declines over time in this example.

Table 1.1 The impact of gearing on growth

	Annual cash flows (£) Year											Average growth (% p.a.)
	0	1	2	3	4	5	6	7	8	9	10	
Example 1												
Basic income	100	110	121	133	146	161	177	195	214	236	259	10.0
Fixed deduction	20	20	20	20	20	20	20	20	20	20	20	–
Residual income	80	90	101	113	126	141	157	175	194	216	239	11.6
Example 2												
Basic income	100	110	121	133	146	161	177	195	214	236	259	10.0
Fixed deduction	50	50	50	50	50	50	50	50	50	50	50	–
Residual income	50	60	71	83	96	111	127	145	164	186	209	15.4
Example 3												
Basic income	100	110	121	133	146	161	177	195	214	236	259	10.0
Fixed deduction	80	80	80	80	80	80	80	80	80	80	80	–
Residual income	20	30	41	53	66	81	97	115	134	156	179	24.5
Example 4												
Basic income	100	90	81	73	66	59	53	48	43	39	35	–10.0
Fixed deduction	20	20	20	20	20	20	20	20	20	20	20	–
Residual income	80	70	61	53	46	39	33	28	23	19	15	–15.4
Example 5												
Basic income	100	90	81	73	66	59	53	48	43	39	35	–10.0
Fixed deduction	50	50	50	50	50	50	50	50	50	50	50	–
Residual income	50	40	31	23	16	9	3	–2	–7	–11	–15	?

Gearing can enhance growth, but it also increases risk. If the growth rate of the basic income is negative, the effect of gearing is to increase the rate of decline, from −10% per annum in the basic income to −15.4% (see Example 4). In fact, as the basic income declines, the gearing ratio rises each year, thus exacerbating the rate of decline. Although the initial gearing ratio is the same in both Examples 1 and 4, the average rate of negative growth of the residual income in Example 4 is greater than the average rate of growth in Example 1. Necessarily, the higher the gearing ratio, the greater the risk of a residual cash flow turning negative (Example 5).

So, whenever a fixed amount is deducted from a variable income, the volatility of the residual is increased. If the deduction were to rise or fall at the same rate as the basic income, the residual would vary at the same rate. Thus, a major factor affecting the volatility of a company's earnings (net profits) over the economic cycle is the company's *operational gearing*; that is, the extent to which its costs are fixed or vary with income from sales. For many businesses, labour costs, rent and rates tend to vary little with income in the short term, and if these costs are a substantial proportion of sales revenue, then they will introduce a significant gearing effect on the company's earnings. In times of rising sales, profits will rise faster than sales income, and vice versa in times of falling sales.

The other principal form of gearing that affects corporate profits is *financial gearing*, defined here as the proportion of a company's capital that is debt rather than equity. With interest payments on debt being a fixed (or relatively stable) prior charge on corporate income, financial gearing will also raise the volatility of the residual earnings, as illustrated above. The combined effect of operational and financial gearing on the growth and volatility of corporate earnings can be very significant. Gearing and its effects are ubiquitous in business and finance.

GEARING IN PROPERTY INVESTMENT

The concept of gearing is equally relevant to property investment. Some investments are inherently geared. A good example is a traditional head leasehold investment in which a fixed head rent is paid to the freeholder, and sub-leases to occupiers allow for regular rent reviews to rental value. In such a case, the head tenant's 'profit rent' is bound to grow (or decline) at a rate faster than the growth of sub-rental income, because the head rent is a fixed deduction from the variable sub-rental income.

The long-term growth record of commercial property and the relative stability of rental income (partly a result of the UK tradition of upward-only rent reviews) have made property a particularly suitable medium for exploiting the potential benefit of gearing. In order to illustrate the impact that gearing may have on returns from property investment, we shall now consider an example of a freehold property costing £1.0m, recently let at its rental value of £50,000 net and subject to rent reviews at five-year intervals. We shall assume that the investor intends to hold for a ten-year period, and is anticipating growth averaging 6% per annum on both rental and capital value. We shall also assume that the investor decides to part-finance the purchase with £700,000 of debt at a fixed interest rate of 6½% per annum, with capital repayable in a lump sum out of the sale proceeds in Year 10. All cash flows are assumed to occur annually in arrears.

The expected cash flows are shown in Table 1.2. Line (1) shows the purchase price (Year 0), the rental income per annum in Years 1 to 5, the rent in Years 6 to 10 after benefiting from growth and a rent review, and the expected sale price in Year 10, having also benefited from 6% growth per annum. Line (2) represents the debt; the capital borrowed in Year 0 and repaid in Year 10, and the annual interest payments in Years 1 to 10. Line (3) is the residual after deducting line (2) from line (1), and represents the expected cash flow of the investor's equity. The investor provides £300,000 of his/her own capital and will receive the residual rent and sale proceeds after interest and capital repayments have been met.

Table 1.2 shows that the property's expected cash flow represents an average annual return of 10.5% over the ten-year period, but through gearing the investment with debt, the investor expects to receive 15.8% per annum on his/her equity capital. By borrowing a substantial part of the capital invested, at an interest rate below the return expected from the property, the investor expects to enhance his/her return beyond what would be received if the investment had been ungeared – that is, if it had been financed by equity capital alone. Note that the returns shown in Table 1.2 are Internal Rates of Return (IRR), the calculation of which is explained in Chapter 3.

The *capital* gearing ratio (loan to value ratio) in this example is 70% (£700,000:£1,000,000) and the initial *income* gearing ratio is 91%

Table 1.2 The impact of gearing on returns

		Expected cash flows (£) Years				*IRR p.a. (%)*
		0	*1–5*	*6–10*	*10*	
Property	(1)	–1,000,000	+50,000	+66,911	+1,790,847	10.5 return
Debt	(2)	+700,000	–45,500	–45,500	–700,000	6.5 cost
Equity	(3)	–300,000	+4,500	+21,411	+1,090,847	15.8 return

(£45,500:£50,000). High gearing can enhance equity returns, but at the cost of increased risk. To illustrate the risk, we now assume (see Table 1.3) that the expected rental growth rate of 6% per annum is achieved for the first five years of the investment only, after which the rental value remains static. We shall also assume that the lack of growth results in a rise in the property's yield to 7% and hence a terminal value (exit value) in Year 10 of £955,871.

The effect of the lower terminal value is to reduce the property's return to 5.4% per annum and, more drastically, to reduce the return on the investor's equity to 2.8% per annum. With the return from the property falling below the cost of debt (6.5%), the gearing has worked to the investor's disadvantage. Compared with the investor's expectations, the property's return has fallen by about 50%, and the return on equity by over 80%. Gearing increases the volatility of returns to equity capital.

It would be easy to imagine circumstances that would have produced a negative return to equity in this case; for example, if rental value had fallen after Year 5 instead of remaining stable, or if the property's terminal value had fallen further, or if rental income had been reduced by tenant default. The risk of financial gearing is also increased if debt is raised on a variable rate basis. A rise in the interest rate payable would have caused a further decline in the equity cash flow.

Investment decisions are made for the future, and the future is always unknown and risky. Investment decisions can only be based on expectations, in the knowledge that future returns, inflation and even taxation are likely to vary from what was expected. Risk is unavoidable in investment, and while allowances can be built into investment appraisals, risk cannot be eradicated, however sophisticated the analysis may be. This has been nicely illustrated by the collapse in share prices over the period 2000–03. At the time of writing, UK share prices have fallen by about 50% from their peak in 2000, prior to which the consensus view among equity analysts was that the risk of shares had declined sharply over the previous two decades.

Table 1.3 The impact of gearing on risk

		Expected cash flows (£) Years				*IRR p.a. (%)*
		0	*1–5*	*6–10*	*10*	
Property	(1)	–1,000,000	+50,000	+66,911	+955,871	5.4 return
Debt	(2)	+700,000	–45,500	–45,500	–700,000	6.5 cost
Equity	(3)	–300,000	+4,500	+21,411	+255,871	2.8 return

SUMMARY

This introduction to cash flow analysis has illustrated the power of compounding to translate relatively modest annual rates of return into multiple changes in value over time. It has also illustrated how an investment's underlying growth can be supplemented by gearing, and how gearing increases risk. The chapter has also emphasised the importance of distinguishing gross returns from net of tax returns, and returns which assume that income is reinvested from returns where annual income is withdrawn for consumption. Over lengthy periods, it is also important to take into account inflation (or deflation), so that the compound rate and growth multiple reflect the real purchasing power of money, and not merely its nominal value.

2

The Time Value of Money: Compounding and Discounting

OVERVIEW

This chapter explains the need to take into account the time value of money in investment appraisal, and demonstrates how this is done by the processes of discounting and compounding. Specifically, the chapter:

- demonstrates the flaws in traditional methods of investment decision-making;
- identifies the principal factors that determine the appropriate discount rate or compound rate to use in cash flow appraisal;
- illustrates the use of compounding to calculate the future value of a present capital sum;
- illustrates the use of discounting to calculate the present value of a sum of money receivable in the future;
- explains how to calculate the future value and present value of a stream of income; and
- explains how to calculate the equivalent annual rate of return from a rate applicable to a shorter sub-period, and to calculate a sub-period rate of return equivalent to an annual rate.

TRADITIONAL APPRAISAL METHODS AND THEIR FLAWS

We start our investigation of appraisal techniques by examining two traditional decision-making methods:

- Payback Period; and
- Average Return.

Both of these methods are badly flawed, particularly in the simplistic form illustrated below. However, an examination of these methods highlights nicely the essential requirements of valid appraisal methods that are the subject of this book. The traditional methods will be explained by means of a simple example involving the selection of a capital investment project by an industrial company.

Investment can be categorised as either *portfolio investment* or *capital investment*. The former would include the purchase of existing investments such as equity shares or bonds, whereas the latter is in the nature of a project involving enterprise; for example, where an industrialist establishes a new manufacturing operation. In the property context, the purchase of a fully-let standing property is portfolio investment, while undertaking a development project would be capital investment. The appraisal techniques examined in this book are appropriate to both types of investment but, at least initially, our examples feature simple capital projects.

Example 2.1: Projects A and B

A company wishes to select the more profitable of two possible projects, A and B. For each project, the initial costs and future net cash flows (income less expenditure in each year) have been estimated carefully (see Table 2.1). Which, if either, project should be selected? Note that, for simplicity, the cash flow figures in the table have been kept unrealistically low. In reality, the figures would be likely to be in thousands or millions of pounds.

Payback Period Method

Using the Payback Period method in its simplest form, projects are selected or rejected according to the length of time needed to repay the initial capital invested. When choosing one from a number of alternatives, the project

Table 2.1 Projects A and B

	Expected cash flows (£)						
	Year						
	0	*1*	*2*	*3*	*4*	*5*	*6*
Project A	−100	+20	+30	+50	+40	–	–
Project B	−100	+40	+30	+20	+10	+50	+50

selected would be the one that repays the capital earliest, provided this is within the company's required payback period.

In our example, the initial outlay is £100 for both projects. From Table 2.1, the cumulative net cash inflows from Project A are expected to amount to £100 by the end of Year 3, but in Project B the initial capital will not be repaid until the end of Year 4. Therefore, using the Payback Period criterion, Project A would be selected, provided that a three-year payback is acceptable to the company.

Average Return Method

In it simplest form, the Average Return method involves the calculation of the average annual return over the expected life of the project. The project that provides the highest return as a percentage of the initial cost would be considered the better investment.

From Table 2.1, Project A is expected to earn a total of £140 over four years. This is an average of £35.00 per annum – 35% of the initial outlay. Project B is expected to earn a total of £200 over six years. This is an average return of £33.33 per annum – 33.3% of the initial outlay.

Provided that a 35% average return is acceptable to the company, then, on this criterion, Project A would again be selected, because its average annual return is a higher percentage of its initial cost than for Project B.

However, these two decision criteria have a number of fatal flaws:

- First, the payback criterion takes no account of the value of cash flows earned after the end of the payback period. Clearly, these are particularly valuable in the case of Project B, and should be taken into account in the selection.
- Second, the average return method does not allow for the replacement of capital invested. For example, a project earning cash inflows averaging 30% per annum of the initial capital investment over three years has not even recouped the initial capital outlay. It would be unprofitable.
- Third, neither method takes proper account of the life of the projects. For example, a project earning an average return of 20% per annum for three years would be preferred to one earning 19% per annum for twenty years.
- Fourth, neither method takes properly into account the time value of money. Money received now is worth more than the same amount of money received in a year's time. Hence, the timing of cash flows is important. In the Payback Period method, the relatively high income of Project B early in its payback period has not been taken into account, compared with Project A, where relatively high returns are made later in its payback period. In the Average Return method, the timing of cash flows is completely ignored.

In the example above, the Payback Period and Average Return methods have been illustrated in their simplest forms. In particular, the Average Return method would normally be based on accounting profit rather than net cash flow each year. That should reduce its unreliability but, even so, it remains fundamentally flawed. The Payback Period criterion is frequently used, sometimes in a more sophisticated form or to back-up a discounted cash flow appraisal. In such cases, it may have some merit as a rule-of-thumb for risky projects in which future returns are particularly difficult to forecast. None the less, it is essentially invalid and has been blamed for short-termism and under-investment in UK industry.

Our example has served to emphasise certain requirements of a valid decision-making criterion; namely, the need to take into account:

- the replacement of capital outlay;
- the amount of cash flows over the whole life of the investment; and
- the timing of cash flows.

These issues are taken into account in discounted cash flow (DCF) methods of appraisal, and are crucial because they are necessary to quantify accurately the profitability of investments. An underlying assumption throughout this book is that, ultimately, investors are primarily concerned with risk and return; that is, they seek high return and low risk. Hence, it is important that return and risk are reflected accurately in the appraisal.

The pursuit of high return and low risk is stated more simply as the aim of maximising investors' wealth. This is an assumption underlying the analysis throughout this book. More specifically, where the investor is a company, the objective is assumed to be the maximisation of value to shareholders and, in the case of investing institutions, such as life assurance and pension funds, the maximisation of value to beneficiaries – that is, policyholders and pensioners.

THE TIME VALUE OF MONEY

The time value of money is fundamental to cash-flow appraisal: £100 received today is worth more than £100 receivable in a year's time. But how much more? We shall address two questions:

(1) How much would you require in a year's time to persuade you to forgo £100 now?

(2) How much would you be willing to pay now for the promise of £100 in a year's time?

In each case, the answer depends on what return you would require from your investment; the investment of £100 in the first case, and some lesser amount in the second. If the investment medium is the same in each case – say, a corporate bond – the required return percentage would be the same. So, we shall consider what that required return might be, and then proceed to answer the questions above.

Even if the sum receivable in a year's time had been guaranteed by the government and virtually riskless, the required return would have been positive, because:

- a positive return could be obtained by depositing the money in a bank;
- in times of inflation, the purchasing power of money is eroded – in a year's time, the real value of the £100 will be less than it is now; and
- access to the money will be lost for the duration of the investment; it will not be available if needed for another purpose.

We have now identified four factors which determine the return required on the investment, and which provide reasons why we would pay less than £100 for a sum of £100 receivable in a year's time. These factors are:

- the returns available on alternative investments, called the *opportunity cost of capital*;
- the requirement for an extra return to compensate for loss of purchasing power in times of *inflation*;
- the requirement for an extra return to compensate for loss of access to the money, called the *liquidity premium*; and
- the requirement for an extra return to compensate for risk, called the *risk premium*.

Various other factors may affect investors' required returns, and therefore the prices paid for investments, such as the cost of buying or selling, cost of management, or liability to taxation. However, these are ignored in this case. Assuming that the investment is offered by a commercial company and subject to risk, the return required might be estimated as follows:

Opportunity cost of liquid, riskless capital (nil inflation), say	2.0%
Extra return to compensate for, say, 2½% inflation rate	2.5%
Liquidity premium, say	1.0%
Risk premium, say	4.5%
	10.0%

In this case, 10% is assumed to be the appropriate required return, or risk-adjusted discount rate (RADR). But, strictly speaking, the relationship between the required return and its components is not additive, but 'chain-linked' as follows:

$$r = (1 + r_f)\,(1 + r_i)\,(1 + r_l)\,(1 + r_p) - 1$$

where = r_f, r_i, r_l, r_p represent the four components above.

Therefore, the required return that is consistent with the figures allocated to the components above would be:

$$\begin{aligned} r &= (1 + 0.02)\,(1 + 0.025)\,(1 + 0.01)\,(1 + 0.045) - 1 \\ &= 10.35\% \end{aligned}$$

In reality, it is difficult to quantify accurately the values of the components, hence the chain-linked approach is pedantic and unhelpful.

On the assumption of a required return of 10% per annum, we can now proceed to answer the two questions above (p. 12). The answer to (1) is simple. The sum required in a year's time is £110. This is the amount that would give an investor a 10% return on the £100 invested. Assuming a required return of 10% per annum, £110 is the *future value* in one year's time which is equivalent to £100 receivable now (*present value*). In effect, we have applied the *compound interest* formula:

$$FV = PV \times (1 + r)^n \tag{2.1}$$

where FV = future value
PV = present value
r = required rate of return per period (decimal)
n = number of periods.

By applying the above formula we get:

$$\begin{aligned} FV &= £100\,(1 + 0.1)^1 \\ &= £100 \times 1.1 \\ &= £110 \end{aligned}$$

Instead of deriving a future value from a present value, Question 2 requires the reverse – a present value to be derived from a future value. This is found by using the *discounting formula*, which is merely the reciprocal of the compounding formula; see Equation (2.2) below:

$$PV = FV \times \frac{1}{(1 + r)^n} \tag{2.2}$$

In Question 2, the future value is £100 and the period is one year, so $n = 1$. The required rate of return is 10% per annum; so $r = 0.1$.

$$PV = £100 \times \frac{1}{(1 + 0.1)^1}$$
$$= £90.91$$

£90.91 is the present value (or discounted value) of £100 receivable in one year using a 10% discount rate. In discounted cash-flow appraisal, the appropriate discount rate is the investor's required rate of return per period – one year, in this case.

This example illustrates the time value of money. It implies that the investor considers £90.91 received now to be equivalent to £100 received in one year. That is because £90.91 is the price that will give the investor the 10% return required.

The result can be checked by calculating the investor's return (£100 – £90.91) as a percentage of the capital invested. That is:

$$\frac{(100 - 90.91) \times 100}{90.91} = 10\%$$

We can now take the application of simple compounding and discounting a stage further by converting our original questions to a three-year time-scale.

(3) How much would you require in three years' time to persuade you to forgo £100 now?

Using the same required return and applying the compounding formula (Equation (2.1)):

$$FV = PV \times (1 + r)^n$$
$$= £100\,(1 + 0.1)^3$$
$$= £133.10$$

£133.10 is the equivalent value in three years' time of £100 now, assuming a required return of 10% per annum (the compound rate).

(4) How much would you be willing to pay now for the promise of £100 in three years' time?

Applying the discounting formula (Equation (2.2)):

$$PV = FV \times \frac{1}{(1 + r)^n}$$

$$= £100 \times \frac{1}{(1 + 0.1)^3}$$

$$= £75.13$$

£75.13 is the present value of £100 receivable in three years' time, assuming a required return of 10% per annum (the discount rate); £75.13 is the price that will give the investor an annual return of 10% over the three years.

COMPOUNDING AND DISCOUNTING CASH FLOWS

Instead of compounding and discounting single sums of money, it is a further short step to apply the techniques to a cash flow – a periodic stream of income or expenditure. Here, we shall consider an income (annuity) of £100 per annum for three years, and calculate its future value (at the end of year three) and its present value. We shall assume that the money is received at the end of each year, and that the required return is 10% per annum, as before.

Again, we shall pose two questions:

(5) How much would you require in three years' time in return for your promise to pay an annuity of £100 per annum for the next three years?

(6) How much would you be willing to pay now to receive an annuity of £100 per annum for the next three years?

Future Value of Annuity

The future value of this annuity is the sum of the future values of each year's income treated separately, so we can calculate these and add them together.

FV of £100 paid in Year 1 = $£100 \times (1 + 0.1)^2$ = £121
FV of £100 paid in Year 2 = $£100 \times (1 + 0.1)^1$ = £110
FV of £100 paid in Year 3 = £100
FV of annuity = £331

£331 received in Year 3 would provide a return of 10% per annum on the annuity paid over the three years.

Note that, as the income is received at the end of each year, and that the future value is calculated at the end of Year 3, the Year 1 income is compounded over two years, the Year 2 income is compounded over one year, and the Year 3 income is not compounded at all, as it is received on the same date as the future value is calculated.

A less laborious way of calculating the future value of an annuity is to apply Equation (2.3):

$$FV \text{ of annuity} = \text{income per period} \times \frac{(1+r)^n - 1}{r} \tag{2.3}$$

Applying the formula in this case:

$$\begin{aligned} FV \text{ of annuity} &= £100 \times \frac{(1+0.1)^3 - 1}{0.1} \\ &= £100 \times 3.31 \\ &= £331 \end{aligned}$$

Present Value of Annuity

The present value of this annuity is merely the sum of the present values of each year's income, so we can calculate these separately and add them together.

$$\begin{aligned} PV \text{ of } £100 \text{ in Year 1} &= £100 \times \frac{1}{(1+0.1)^1} = £\ \ 90.91 \\ PV \text{ of } £100 \text{ in Year 2} &= £100 \times \frac{1}{(1+0.1)^2} = £\ \ 82.64 \\ PV \text{ of } £100 \text{ in Year 3} &= £100 \times \frac{1}{(1+0.1)^3} = £\ \ 75.13 \\ PV \text{ of annuity} & \qquad\qquad\qquad\quad\ = £248.68 \end{aligned}$$

This result means that, if an investor buys this annuity for £248.68, the cash flow of £100 per annum for three years will represent an annual return of 10% on the £248.68 cost over the three-year life of the investment. Note how the discounting process takes into account the time value of money. The present value of £100 receivable in Year 3 is less than the present value of £100 receivable in Year 2, which is less than that receivable in Year 1.

Again, a less laborious way to calculate the present value of an annuity is to apply Equation (2.4):

$$PV \text{ of annuity} = \text{income per period} \times \frac{1 - \left[\dfrac{1}{(1+r)^n}\right]}{r} \qquad (2.4)$$

Applying the formula in this case:

$$\begin{aligned} PV \text{ of annuity} &= £100 \times \frac{1 - \left[\dfrac{1}{(1+0.1)^3}\right]}{0.1} \\ &= £100 \times 2.4868 \\ &= £248.68 \end{aligned}$$

Note

- The future value multiplier (compound factor) in Equation (2.3) is often called the Amount of £1 per annum;
- The present value multiplier (discount factor) in Equation (2.4) is often called the Present Value of £1 per annum or Years' Purchase;
- A neater representation of the formula for calculating the discount factor in Equation (2.4) is:

$$\frac{1-(1+r)^{-n}}{r}$$

THE CONCEPT OF PRESENT VALUE

In the final case shown above, we calculated the present value of the cash flow to be £248.68 by discounting the future income, using the required return as the discount rate. The case was simplified by its brief (three-year) time-scale and its fixed income, but the general concept is universal to income-earning investments, and applicable to a variety of contexts. The general concept is that: *the value of an investment is the present (discounted) value of the expected future cash flow to be generated by the investment.*

Alternatively, we could express the concept as: *the value of an investment is determined by investors' required return, expected future cash flow and the passage of time over which the cash flow is generated.* The concept is represented by Equations (2.5) and (2.6), the latter being an alternative representation of the former:

$$PV = \frac{C_1}{(1+r)} + \frac{C_2}{(1+r)^2} + \frac{C_3}{(1+r)^3} + \dots\dots\dots + \frac{C_n}{(1+r)^n} \qquad (2.5)$$

$$PV = \sum_{t=1}^{n} \frac{C_t}{(1+r)^t} \qquad (2.6)$$

where PV = present value
r = investor's required return per period
$C_{1,2,3,n}$ = expected cash flows in periods 1,2,3,n
t = time period from 1 to n.

The Present Value equation and its concept are of fundamental importance to property investment, and relevant to:

- the valuation and appraisal of investments;
- investment decision-making; and
- understanding the determination of market prices.

The equation can be applied to a wide range of investments:

- of any duration;
- with positive or negative cash flow;
- whether the cash flow is fixed or variable;
- in nominal terms or real terms;
- secure or risky;
- gross or net of tax; or
- using time periods of less or more than one year.

However, the discounting must be consistent with the cash flow in terms of timing and frequency. For example, if the cash flow is paid quarterly, the discounting must also be based on quarterly periods.

PERIODIC EQUIVALENT RATES OF RETURN

So far, our examples have assumed that income is received in one annual payment at the end of the year. However, an investment may pay income more frequently – say, monthly or quarterly – so, here the cash flow must be discounted at a monthly or quarterly rate. However, a sub-period rate of return is not a simple fraction of the annual rate, because of the time value of money. The quarterly rate of return equivalent to a 10% annual rate must be less than 2½%. First, we shall work through an example to calculate the annual interest rate that is equivalent to a monthly rate.

Example 2.2: Annualising a Sub-period Interest Rate

Mr Green's bank account is £100 overdrawn at the start of the year. He does not repay any debt over the year. The bank charges interest on the amount overdrawn at the end of the previous month at a rate of 1% per month. What is the annual equivalent rate charged?

At the end of the first month, Mr Green would owe the bank £101 (the £100 debt plus £1 interest). In the second month, the interest charged would be 1% of £101, an amount marginally greater than £1, and so on. We can apply the compound interest formula (Equation (2.1)) to calculate the amount that will be owed to the bank at the end of the year:

$$FV = PV \times (1 + r)^n$$

where PV = £100
r = 0.01
n = 12

Using these values in the compound interest equation, we get:

$$\begin{aligned} FV &= 100\ (1 + 0.01)^{12} \\ &= 100 \times 1.1268 \\ &= £112.68 \end{aligned}$$

The annualised interest charge is £12.68 and the annual equivalent interest rate is 12.68%. Formally, the annual rate of interest is calculated from Equation (2.7):

$$\text{Annual rate of interest} = (1 + r_s)^n - 1 \qquad (2.7)$$

where r_s = sub-period rate (decimal)
n = number of sub-periods per annum

Substituting the values from this example into Equation (2.7):

$$\begin{aligned} &= (1 + 0.01)^{12} - 1 \\ &= 1.1268 - 1 \\ &= 0.1268 \\ &= 12.68\% \end{aligned}$$

The annualised interest rate charged on the £100 is 12.68%, sometimes called an Annual Equivalent Rate (AER).

Note that the essential difference between Equation (2.7) and Equation

(2.1) is the suffix –1. This is because Equation (2.7) is measuring the incremental value within the period, rather than a compounded value at the end of the period.

The converse of annualising a sub-period rate of return is calculating an equivalent sub-period rate from an annual rate. The relevant formula is shown in Equation (2.8):

$$\text{Sub-period rate} = (1 + r_a)^{1/n} - 1 \tag{2.8}$$

where r_a = annual rate (decimal)
n = number of sub-periods per annum

Example 2.3: Calculating an Equivalent Quarterly Rate from an Annual Interest Rate

What quarterly rate of interest is equivalent to an annual rate of 12%?

$$\begin{aligned}\text{Quarterly rate} &= (1 + 0.12)^{1/4} - 1 \\ &= 0.02874 \\ &= 2.87\%\end{aligned}$$

It is important to understand that the quarterly equivalent rate must be less than a quarter of the annual rate because of the time value of money: £100 compounding at 2.87% per quarter will amount to £112 at the year end, equivalent to an annual rate of 12%.

A fundamental rule of cash-flow appraisal is that the compounding or discounting process must be consistent with the frequency and timing of the cash flow. But, when compounding or discounting a capital sum over a period which is not a discrete number of years, it is not necessary to convert the annual rate to the equivalent sub-period rate, provided that the exponent (*n* in the formulae) is consistent with the compound or discount rate used (see Example 2.4).

Example 2.4

What is the present value of £100 receivable in 15 months, assuming a required return of 12% per annum?

$$PV = £100 \times \frac{1}{(1 + r)^n}$$

(a) Based on the quarterly rate calculated in Example 2.3:

$$PV = £100 \times \frac{1}{(1 + 0.02874)^5} = £86.79$$

(b) Based on the annual rate of 12%:

$$PV = £100 \times \frac{1}{(1 + 0.12)^{1.25}} = £86.79$$

SUMMARY

The principal aim of this chapter has been to explain the time value of money: what it represents, its significance in investment appraisal, and how it is taken into account in the compounding and discounting process. Although the chapter has concentrated on concepts, it is important that the reader understands the calculations introduced, because these underpin the appraisal techniques to be introduced in Chapter 3, and developed subsequently throughout the book. The reader should also note the assumption underlying the analysis throughout the book – that the ultimate objective is to maximise investors' wealth.

SELF-ASSESSMENT QUESTIONS

2.1 (a) Table 2.2 shows the expected annual net cash flows arising from a decision to take on projects P and Q. If one of the projects were to be undertaken, which project would be chosen, using:

- the Payback Period method; and
- the Average Return method.

(b) Which project do you think is to be preferred, and why?

Table 2.2 Projects P and Q

	Expected cash flows (£) Year					
	0	*1*	*2*	*3*	*4*	*5*
Project P	−100	+10	+20	+30	+40	+60
Project Q	−100	+50	+40	+30	+20	+10

2.2 What is the present value of a sum of £1,000 receivable in one year's time:

(a) Assuming a required return of 9% per annum?
(b) Assuming a required return of 12% per annum?
(c) Explain why the answer to (b) is lower than the answer to (a).

2.3 Assuming a required return of 8½% per annum,

(a) What sum of money receivable in 5 years' time is equivalent to £10,000 receivable now?
(b) What sum of money receivable now would be equivalent to the answer to (a)?

2.4 What is the present value of £10,000 receivable in 18 months' time, assuming a required return of 2% per quarter?

2.5 Three banks each pay interest of £4 per annum on a £100 deposit, but,
Bank A pays £4 annually in arrears,
Bank B pays £2 six-monthly in arrears, and
Bank C pays £1 quarterly in arrears.
Are these terms equally attractive or, if not, which bank offers the best terms?

2.6 Prove the answer to Question 2.5 by calculating the annual equivalent rate of interest paid by each bank.

2.7 If an investor requires 15% per annum from an investment that pays interest quarterly in arrears, what is the required quarterly rate?

2.8 What is the present value of an investment that is due to pay a total of £1,000 over the coming year in four equal instalments at the end of each quarter? Assume a required return of 15% per annum.

2.9 Assuming now that the investment in Question 2.8 pays interest quarterly in advance, what would its value be? Explain the difference.

ANSWERS TO SELF-ASSESSMENT QUESTIONS

2.1 (a) **Payback Period method**

Project P has a payback period of four years. Project Q has a payback period of less than three years. So, Project Q is preferred on the payback criterion.

Average Return method

Project P has an average return per annum of 32%. Project Q has an average return per annum of 30%. So, Project P is preferred on the average return criterion.

(b) Project P earns a higher total and average return. However, the bulk of this comes in Years 4 and 5. In comparison, the majority of Project Q's return is earned in Years 1 and 2.

Taking into account the time value of money, the early timing of Project Q's income should more than compensate for the higher total income from Project P. However, the correct choice of investment depends on the required return. (Only at rates below 5% would Project P be preferred.)

2.2 (a)
$$£1{,}000 \times \frac{1}{(1 + 0.09)} = £917.43.$$

(b)
$$£1{,}000 \times \frac{1}{(1 + 0.12)} = £892.86.$$

(c) Because the higher discount rate reduces the present value by a greater amount. The discount rate is the investor's required return, and in order to achieve the higher return in (b), the investor will have to pay a lower price than in (a).

2.3 (a) $£10{,}000\,(1 + 0.085)^5 = £15{,}036.57$.
(b) £10,000 (of course!).

2.4
$$£10{,}000 \times \frac{1}{(1 + 0.02)^6} = £8{,}879.71.$$

2.5 Bank C provides the best terms, and Bank A the worst. Money received early is worth more than the same amount of money at a later date. The three banks all pay out the same amount per annum but, on average, Bank C pays it earlier than Bank B, and Bank B earlier than Bank A.

2.6 Bank A $= 4.00\%$ AER.
Bank B: $(1 + 0.02)^2 - 1 = 0.0404 = 4.04\%$ AER.
Bank C: $(1 + 0.01)^4 - 1 = 0.0406 = 4.06\%$ AER.

2.7 $(1 + 0.15)^{1/4} - 1 = 0.0356$
$= 3.56\%$.

2.8 The question can be answered in the following ways:

(a) By discounting each quarter's income at the quarterly equivalent of 15% per annum (calculated in Question 2.7) with the exponents representing quarterly periods:

$$\text{1st quarter: } £250 \times \frac{1}{(1 + 0.0356)} = £241.41$$

$$\text{2nd quarter: } £250 \times \frac{1}{(1 + 0.0356)^2} = £233.11$$

$$\text{3rd quarter: } £250 \times \frac{1}{(1 + 0.0356)^3} = £225.09$$

$$\text{4th quarter: } £250 \times \frac{1}{(1 + 0.0356)^4} = £217.36$$

$$\text{Present value} = £916.97.$$

(b) By discounting each quarter's income using the annual rate of 15% with exponents representing quarterly fractions of years:

$$£250 \times \frac{1}{(1 + 0.15)^{1/4}} = £241.42$$

$$£250 \times \frac{1}{(1 + 0.15)^{1/2}} = £233.13$$

$$£250 \times \frac{1}{(1 + 0.15)^{3/4}} = £225.12$$

$$£250 \times \frac{1}{(1 + 0.15)^{1}} = £217.39$$

$$\text{Present value} = £917.06.$$

(c) By applying the present value of an annuity formula (Equation (2.4)), using the quarterly equivalent of 15% (calculated in Question 2.7):

$$PV = £250 \times \frac{1 - \left[\dfrac{1}{(1 + r)^n}\right]}{r}$$

$$= £250 \times \frac{1 - \left[\frac{1}{(1 + 0.0356)^4}\right]}{0.0356}$$

$$= £916.96.$$

The small differences in the three answers result from rounding error.

2.9 Using the method in Question 2.8(a) above:

$$\text{1st quarter: } £250 \times 1 = £250$$

$$\text{2nd quarter: } £250 \times \frac{1}{(1 + 0.0356)} = £241.41$$

$$\text{3rd quarter: } £250 \times \frac{1}{(1 + 0.0356)^2} = £233.11$$

$$\text{4th quarter: } £250 \times \frac{1}{(1 + 0.0356)^3} = £225.09$$

$$\text{Value} = £949.61.$$

The value is enhanced because, on average, the income is received earlier. The first quarter's income is received immediately, so it is not discounted at all. The second quarter's income is received at the start of the second quarter (which equals the end of the first quarter). The third quarter's income is discounted over two quarters, and the fourth quarter's income is discounted over three quarters.

The discounting process must be consistent with the cash flow in all respects, including frequency and timing.

3

Investment Decision-making by Discounted Cash Flow

OVERVIEW

Drawing on the introduction to compounding and discounting in Chapter 2, this chapter introduces and explains the application of three methods of making investment decisions, each of which takes into account the time value of money. These are:

- the net present value (NPV);
- the net terminal value (NTV); and
- the internal rate of return (IRR).

These are demonstrated using the example of Projects A and B introduced in Chapter 2. This is repeated below for ease of reference.

Example 3.1: Projects A and B

A company wants to select the more profitable of two possible projects. It has estimated carefully the initial costs and future net cash flows for each project, as shown in Table 3.1.

THE NET PRESENT VALUE (NPV)

The Concept of the NPV

The net present value (NPV) is the sum of all cash flows (both negative and positive) expected from taking on a project, discounted back to the present.

Table 3.1 Projects A and B

	Expected cash flows (£) Year						
	0	*1*	*2*	*3*	*4*	*5*	*6*
Project A	−100	+20	+30	+50	+40	–	–
Project B	−100	+40	+30	+20	+10	+50	+50

This is expressed in both Equation (3.1) and Equation (3.2), the two equations being alternative representations of the concept.

$$NPV = \sum_{t=0}^{n} \frac{C_t}{(1 + r)^t} \tag{3.1}$$

$$NPV = C_0 + \frac{C_1}{(1 + r)} + \frac{C_2}{(1 + r)^2} + \ldots\ldots\ldots + \frac{C_n}{(1 + r)^n} \tag{3.2}$$

where n is the number of periods to the end of the project;
t is the time period 0 to n;
$C_{0,1,2,n}$ is the expected cash flow in periods 0, 1, 2, n;
r is the investor's required rate of return per period (discount rate); and
Σ represents summation.

The difference between Equations (3.1) and (3.2) and the present value equations introduced in Chapter 2 (Equations (2.5) and (2.6)) is that the NPV also takes into account the initial cost of the investment in period 0. The NPV takes into account all expected income and expenditure arising from a decision to take on the investment (represented in the cash flows), together with the investor's required return to cover the cost of capital and compensate for risk and so on (represented in the discount rate). Therefore, the NPV is an expected financial surplus (or deficit) above (or below) the return required on the capital invested.

The NPV decision rule follows from the above. Projects with a nil or positive NPV should be accepted. Projects with a negative NPV should be rejected. When selecting one out of a number of alternative (mutually exclusive) projects, the project with the highest positive NPV should be chosen.

Application of the NPV Method

We shall now calculate the NPVs for Projects A and B, and decide whether the projects should be accepted or rejected. Assume that the investor's required return is 15% per annum in each case.

Project A

Inserting the Project A figures into Equation (3.2) gives:

$$NPV = -100 + \frac{20}{(1 + 0.15)} + \frac{30}{(1 + 0.15)^2} + \frac{50}{(1 + 0.15)^3} + \frac{40}{(1 + 0.15)^4}$$

$$= -100 + (0.870 \times 20) + (0.756 \times 30) + (0.658 \times 50) + (0.572 \times 40)$$
$$= -100 + 17.39 + 22.68 + 32.88 + 22.87$$
$$= -£4.18$$

The effect of the equation is to multiply the cash flow for each year by a factor, known as the discount factor, given by applying Equation (3.3):

$$\text{Discount Factor} = \frac{1}{(1 + r)^t} \quad (3.3)$$

It is often more convenient, particularly in the case of a multi-period project, to set the calculation out in a table, as shown in Table 3.2 for Project A.

Table 3.2 Project A – calculating the NPV

Year	*Cash flow (£)*	*Discount factor @ 15% p.a.*	*Discounted cash flow (£)*
0	–100	1.000	–100.00
1	+20	0.870	+17.39
2	+30	0.756	+22.68
3	+50	0.658	+32.88
4	+40	0.572	+22.87
			NPV = –4.18

In the case of Project A, the initial cost is greater than the discounted sum of the future cash flow. The negative NPV signifies that the project should be rejected. It is insufficiently profitable and is not expected to provide the 15% per annum return required.

Project B

A similar calculation is now undertaken for Project B, as shown in Table 3.3. At the required return of 15%, the NPV of Project B is positive. The project should be selected, because it is expected to provide a surplus over and above the 15% per annum return required on the capital invested.

Note that the NPV method selects Project B, whereas both traditional methods selected Project A.

Table 3.3 Project B – calculating the NPV

Year	*Cash flow (£)*	*Discount factor @ 15% p.a.*	*Discounted cash flow (£)*
0	–100	1.000	–100.00
1	+40	0.870	+34.80
2	+30	0.756	+22.68
3	+20	0.658	+13.16
4	+10	0.572	+5.72
5	+50	0.497	+24.85
6	+50	0.432	+21.60
			NPV = +22.81

THE NET TERMINAL VALUE (NTV)

The Concept of the NTV

The net terminal value (NTV) is an alternative decision criterion to the NPV. It is less commonly used, but is included here because it is a useful tool in the appraisal of real estate development, and because its study adds to a fuller understanding of cash-flow appraisal methods.

The NTV concept is similar to that of the NPV, but instead of discounting future cash flows back to the present, future cash flows are compounded forward to the end of the project. It is compounded cash flow rather than discounted cash flow, and is expressed by both Equations (3.4) and (3.5).

$$NTV = \sum_{t=0}^{n} (1 + r)^{n-t} \times C_t \tag{3.4}$$

$$NTV = C_0 (1 + r)^n + C_1 (1 + r)^{n-1} + \dots\dots\dots\dots + C_n \tag{3.5}$$

In Equation (3.5), as in Equation (3.2), the cash flow for each year is multiplied by a factor. In this case, it is the *compound factor* given by Equation (3.6):

$$\text{Compound factor} = (1 + r)^{n-t} \qquad (3.6)$$

Notice that, in this case, the Year 0 cash flow is multiplied by the largest factor, and the factor then reduces to 1 by the final year of the project. The cash flow in the final year is not compounded because, as cash flows are assumed to be received annually in arrears, this last cash flow would be received on the day that the NTV is calculated; that is, at the end of the project's life.

Like the NPV, the NTV is a financial surplus (or deficit) above (or below) the minimum return required to make the project worthwhile. The decision rule is similar to the NPV. All projects with a nil or positive NTV should be accepted. Projects with a negative NTV should be rejected. When selecting from a number of alternative projects, the one with the highest positive NTV should be chosen.

Application of the NTV Method

We shall now calculate the NTV for Projects A and B, and so decide whether the projects should be accepted or rejected. As before, the investor's required return is 15%. Table 3.4 shows the calculations for Project A. The negative NTV means that the sum of the compounded cash flows is negative, and the project should be rejected, because it is not expected to provide the 15% per annum return required. We now do the same calculation for Project B, as shown in Table 3.5. The positive NTV here indicates that Project B should be selected.

Table 3.4 Project A – calculating the NTV

Year	*Cash flow (£)*	*Compound factor @ 15% p.a.*	*Compounded cash flow (£)*
0	–100	1.749	–174.90
1	+20	1.521	+30.42
2	+30	1.323	+39.68
3	+50	1.150	+57.50
4	+40	1	+40.00
			NTV = –7.30

Table 3.5 Project B – calculating the NTV

Year	*Cash flow (£)*	*Compound factor @ 15% p.a.*	*Compounded cash flow (£)*
0	–100	2.313	–231.31
1	+40	2.011	+80.45
2	+30	1.749	+52.47
3	+20	1.521	+30.42
4	+10	1.323	+13.23
5	+50	1.150	+57.50
6	+50	1	+50.00
			NTV = +52.76

The NTV criterion selects and rejects the same projects as the NPV method. The concept of the two methods is essentially the same. Both measure the expected surplus above (or below, if negative) the required rate of return. The difference is that the surplus is being measured at different points in time.

This can be illustrated in the case of Project B above. The NPV measures the surplus at year 0, the NTV at year 6. So, if the NTV is discounted at the investor's required rate of return over the six-year life of the project, the outcome should be the NPV. You might like to check this out for yourself.

THE INTERNAL RATE OF RETURN (IRR)

The Concept and Calculation of the IRR

The internal rate of return (IRR) measures the rate of return that the investment earns on the capital invested. The decision rule for project appraisal is that the project should be selected if the expected IRR equals or exceeds the investor's required rate of return. If it does not, the project should be rejected.

We can view the IRR as either:

- the discount rate which, when applied to a project's cash flow, results in a nil NPV; or
- the compound rate that will result in a nil NTV.

Therefore, the IRR is the solution to r in either the NPV or the NTV equation, where the NPV or NTV = 0. Here, we shall use the NPV equation:

$$NPV = \sum_{t=0}^{n} \frac{C_t}{(1 + r)^t} = 0$$

or

$$NPV = C_0 + \frac{C_1}{(1 + r)} + \frac{C_2}{(1 + r)^2} + \ldots\ldots\ldots + \frac{C_n}{(1 + r)^n} = 0$$

Unfortunately, there is no simple way to solve for r in this equation. We must find the IRR by iteration (trial and error) using the following method:

- Estimate the IRR approximately by comparing the project's incoming and outgoing cash flows (see Chapter 4).
- Calculate the NPV using the estimated IRR as a first trial discount rate. If the NPV is negative, the discount rate used is higher than the IRR, so now select a lower trial rate. If the NPV is positive at the first trial rate, that rate is too low, so now select a higher rate.
- Calculate the NPV at the second trial discount rate. If this produces an NPV with a different sign than the first trial rate, then find the IRR by *interpolating* between the two trial rates using the formula shown as Equation (3.7):

$$IRR = r_l + \left[(r_h - r_l) \times \frac{NPV_l}{NPV_l - NPV_h}\right] \tag{3.7}$$

where: r_l is the lower trial discount rate;
r_h is the higher trial discount rate;
NPV_l is the NPV using the lower rate; and
NPV_h is the NPV using the higher rate.

If the NPVs calculated by both trial rates have the same sign, then it is possible to *extrapolate* to find the IRR. It is conventional, however, to select another trial rate that produces an NPV with a different sign, to enable interpolation. This is the method used in this book.

When using interpolation (or extrapolation), we are assuming that there is a linear relationship between the IRR and the NPV. However, the relationship is not linear, hence using linear interpolation to calculate the IRR is not precisely accurate. In fact, calculating the IRR by interpolating between substantially different trial rate parameters can be seriously inaccurate. Trial rates should, therefore, be reasonably close for accuracy.

This is illustrated in Figure 3.1, which shows that the relationship between the NPV and IRR is curved. The curve defines how a project's NPV

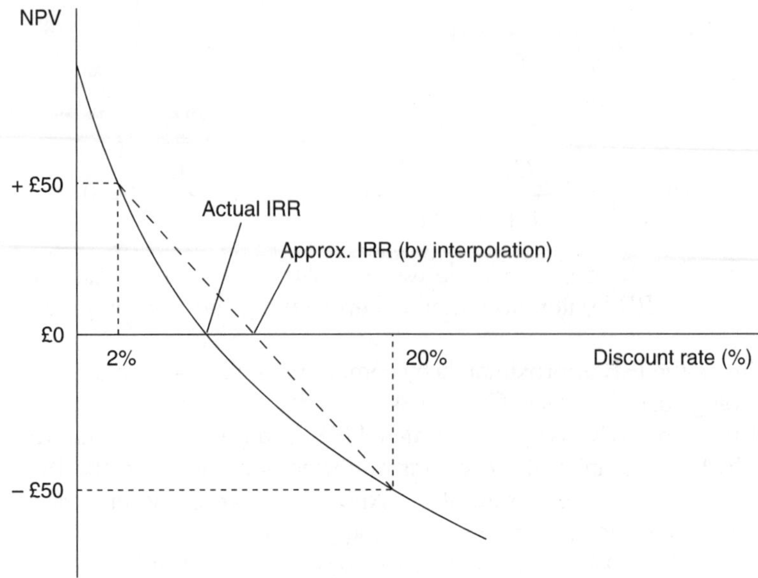

Figure 3.1 *Relationship between NPV and IRR*

varies according to the discount rate used. The project illustrated provides a £50 NPV at a 2% discount rate and an NPV of –£50 at a 20% discount rate. Interpolating between 2% and 20% produces an IRR of 11%, but the actual IRR is significantly less than 11%, as shown by the intersection of the curve with the horizontal axis.

The alternative to calculating the IRR by this manual process is to use a calculator or computer. However, in order to gain an understanding of the IRR, it is important to be able to practise the process described above.

Application of the IRR Method

We shall now calculate the IRRs for Projects A and B, and decide whether the projects should be accepted or rejected, using the IRR criterion.

Project A

Having already calculated that the NPV of Project A is negative at a discount rate of 15% per annum, we know that the IRR must be less than 15%. This is because the IRR is the discount rate that results in a nil NPV, and a lower discount rate must raise the NPV. We shall therefore select a first trial of 12%. The NPV is then calculated as shown in Table 3.6.

Table 3.6 Project A, NPV at 12 per cent

Year	*Cash flow (£)*	*Discount factor @ 12% p.a.*	*Discounted cash flow (£)*
0	−100	1.000	−100.00
1	+20	0.893	+17.86
2	+30	0.797	+23.91
3	+50	0.712	+35.60
4	+40	0.636	+25.44
			NPV @ 12% = +2.81

Table 3.7 Project A, NPV at 14 per cent

Year	*Cash flow (£)*	*Discount factor @ 14% p.a.*	*Discounted cash flow (£)*
0	−100	1.000	−100.00
1	+20	0.877	+17.54
2	+30	0.769	+23.07
3	+50	0.675	+33.75
4	+40	0.592	+23.68
			NPV @ 14% = −1.96

As the NPV is positive using a discount rate of 12%, we know that the IRR must be greater than 12%. Therefore, our second trial rate must be higher than 12% and, in order to interpolate, sufficiently high to produce a negative NPV. We shall use a rate of 14% as shown in Table 3.7. So, at r_l = 12%, NPV_l = £2.81, and at r_h = 14%, NPV_h = −£1.96. Since NPV_l and NPV_h have different signs, we can interpolate using the formula in Equation (3.7):

$$IRR = r_l + \left[(r_h - r_l) \times \frac{NPV_l}{NPV_l - NPV_h} \right]$$

$$= 12 + \left[(14 - 12) \times \frac{2.81}{2.81 - (-1.96)} \right]$$

$$= 12 + \frac{5.62}{4.77}$$

$$IRR = 13.2\%$$

The expected IRR is therefore 13.2%. Since this is below the required return of 15%, the project would be rejected.

Project B

The NPV calculation in Table 3.3 (p. 30) tells us that the IRR is going to be higher than 15%. Therefore, we shall select a first trial rate of 20%.

Table 3.8 Project B – NPV at 20 per cent

Year	*Cash flow (£)*	*Discount factor @ 20% p.a.*	*Discounted cash flow (£)*
0	−100	1.000	−100.00
1	+40	0.833	+33.32
2	+30	0.694	+20.82
3	+20	0.579	+11.58
4	+10	0.482	+4.82
5	+50	0.402	+20.10
6	+50	0.335	+16.75
			NPV @ 20% = +7.39

Table 3.9 Project B, NPV at 24 per cent

Year	*Cash flow (£)*	*Discount factor @ 24% p.a.*	*Discounted cash flow (£)*
0	−100	1.000	−100.00
1	+40	0.806	+32.24
2	+30	0.650	+19.50
3	+20	0.524	+10.48
4	+10	0.423	+4.23
5	+50	0.341	+17.05
6	+50	0.275	+13.75
			NPV @ 24% = −2.75

However, the calculation in Table 3.8 shows that the NPV is still positive at the 20% discount rate – so, the IRR must be higher. The second trial rate is taken as 24%, to obtain a negative NPV for interpolation, as shown in Table 3.9. So, at r_l = 20%, NPV_l = £7.39, and at r_h = 24%, NPV_h = –£2.75. We can now interpolate as follows, using the formula from Equation (3.7):

$$IRR = r_l + \left[(r_h - r_l) \times \frac{NPV_l}{NPV_l - NPV_h} \right]$$

$$= 20 + \left[(24 - 20) \times \frac{7.39}{7.39 - (-2.75)} \right]$$

$$= 20 + \frac{29.56}{10.14}$$

$$IRR = 22.9\%$$

The expected IRR is 22.9%; this exceeds the required return of 15%, so the project would be selected.

SUMMARY

This chapter has explained and demonstrated the calculation of the NPV, NTV and IRR, and their application to investment decision-making. The NPV is the present value (in £s) of the investment's expected cash flow, discounted back to the present at the investor's required rate of return. The NTV is the future value (in £s) of the investment's expected cash flow compounded forward to the termination of the investment at the same rate of return. The IRR is the rate of return which, when used to discount or compound a project's expected cash flow, results in both a nil NPV and a nil NTV. It is also a true measure of the expected rate of return (per cent per period) on the capital invested.

Conceptually, that is a rather neat symmetry, and perhaps deceptively simple. In particular, the IRR is quite complex, both conceptually and mathematically. In practice, the three criteria will normally be calculated using computer software. However, it is important to practice the calculations manually in order to gain a full understanding of the concepts.

SELF-ASSESSMENT QUESTIONS

3.1 Explain briefly what the NPV, NTV and IRR measure and how they differ.

3.2 The NPV decision rule says that an investment with a nil NPV should be accepted. Explain why.

3.3 In the case of conventional investments starting with a negative cash flow and thereafter producing an income, state which of the following statements are true, and which are false.

- In investment appraisal, *ceteris paribus*, the lower the discount rate used, the higher will be the NPV;
- In investment appraisal, *ceteris paribus*, the higher the discount rate used, the lower will be the NPV;
- If the NPV of an investment is negative at a 12% discount rate, the investment's IRR must be less than 12%;
- If the NPV of an investment is positive at a 12% discount rate, the investment's IRR must be greater than 12%.

3.4 Using the concept of the interpolation formula, estimate by mental arithmetic the IRR of Projects R, S and T from the NPV data given.

- Project R's NPV is £100 at a 10% discount rate and –£100 at an 11% discount rate;
- Project S's NPV is £100 at a 10% discount rate and –£200 at a 12% discount rate;
- Project T's NPV is £10 at a 10% discount rate and –£200 at a 13% discount rate.

3.5 Table 3.10 shows the expected annual net cash flows arising from a decision to take on projects P and Q – the same projects as in SAQ 2.1. For both projects, calculate:

- the net present value (NPV);
- the net terminal value (NTV); and
- the internal return rate (IRR).

Table 3.10 Projects P and Q

	Expected cash flows (£) Year					
	0	*1*	*2*	*3*	*4*	*5*
Project P	–100	+10	+20	+30	+40	+60
Project Q	–100	+50	+40	+30	+20	+10

Use the results of the calculations to make an investment decision in each case. Assume that the risk of each project is identical, and that the investor's required return is 17% in each case.

ANSWERS TO SELF-ASSESSMENT QUESTIONS

3.1 Both NPV and NTV measure (in £s) the financial surplus (or deficit) an investment is expected to generate over and above the investor's required return, taking into account the time value of money. The difference is that the NTV measures the surplus at the end of the investment's life, while the NPV measures it at the present time.

Both the NPV and NTV take into account the opportunity cost of capital and the risk of the investment, because those factors are reflected in the discount rate or compound rate used. By contrast, the IRR is merely a rate of return on capital invested, which takes no account of the cost of that capital or risk. Hence, when using the expected IRR as a decision criterion, it needs to be compared with the investment's required return, which does reflect these factors.

3.2 Because a nil NPV still means that the investment is expected to produce a return equal to the required return.

A positive NPV means that the expected return exceeds the required return, and a negative NPV means that the expected return is less than that required.

3.3 All four statements are true.

3.4 *Note*: These answers assume a linear relationship between NPV and IRR. Project R's IRR is easy to estimate. It is 10.5%, because the two NPVs are equidistant above and below nil, and the difference between the two trial rates is 1%.

$$\text{The IRR} = 10\% + (1\% \times \frac{100}{200}) = 10.5\%.$$

Project S's IRR is 10.67%, because it is 10% plus one third of the 2% difference between the two trial rates.

Project T's IRR is difficult to calculate precisely by mental arithmetic but it must be fractionally over 10%, because the NPV is much closer to nil at the 10% discount rate than it is at the 13% discount rate.

$$\text{The IRR} = 10\% + (3\% \times \frac{10}{210}) = 10.14\%.$$

Remember, the IRR is the discount rate that results in a nil NPV.

3.5

	NPV	NTV	IRR
Project P	−£9.39	−£20.60	13.9%
Project Q	+£5.95	+£12.98	20.4%

All three decision criteria (NPV, NTV and IRR) indicate the same decision:

- Reject Project P; and
- Accept Project Q.

Note: Small rounding errors are inevitable in these calculations. However, if you obtain answers substantially different from those above, you should check your calculations carefully by reference to the examples in the text.

4

Understanding the IRR and NPV

OVERVIEW

In Chapter 3, we saw that the IRR of an investment is both:

- the discount rate that results in a nil NPV; and
- the compound rate that results in a nil NTV.

This is certainly true, but it does not provide a full understanding of the IRR as a measure of return. In this chapter, we explore the IRR further, investigate a number of pitfalls in the application of the IRR, and show how these can be overcome. We conclude with a summary of the relative merits of the IRR and NPV methods of appraisal.

UNDERSTANDING THE IRR

In this section, we shall again use the Project A example as an illustration. Project A's expected cash flow is repeated in Table 4.1 for ease of reference.

Table 4.1 Project A

	Expected cash flow (£)				
	Year				
	0	*1*	*2*	*3*	*4*
Project A	−100	+20	+30	+50	+40

In Chapter 3, we found the IRR of Project A to be 13.2% per annum (13.16% is more precise). This means that the cash flow earned through the life of the project is just sufficient to repay all capital invested *and* earn the IRR rate of 13.16% per annum on capital invested before that capital is repaid. These points are illustrated in Table 4.2.

At the outset of the project, Year 0, £100 was invested, as shown on the top line of the Capital outstanding column; 13.16% of £100 is £13.16; so, of the £20 cash flow earned in Year 1, the remainder (£6.84) is notionally available to repay capital invested. At the end of Year 1, therefore, only £93.16 (£100 – £6.84) is notionally outstanding; 13.16% of £93.16 is £12.26 which, when deducted from the second year's cash flow of £30, leaves £17.74 available from that cash flow to repay capital, and so on. The cash flow earned in the last year of the project is just sufficient to pay 13.16% on the remaining capital outstanding before repaying that capital.

The example demonstrates that *the IRR measures the rate of return earned on capital before that capital is repaid.* In calculating a project's IRR, full allowance is made for repayment of the capital invested. This makes the IRR a true measure of return and a valid unit for comparing investments.

In Chapter 2, we used the Average Return method to obtain a return for Project A of 35%, compared with 13.16% using the IRR method. The Average Return percentage was unrealistically high, as it made no allowance for capital repayment.

Table 4.2 Project A, explaining the IRR

Year	*Cash flow earned (£)*		*13.16% of capital outstanding*		*Capital outstanding (£)*	*End of year*
					100.00	0
1	20	–	13.16	=	6.84	
					93.16	1
2	30	–	12.26	=	17.74	
					75.42	2
3	50	–	9.93	=	40.07	
					35.35	3
4	40	–	4.65	=	35.35	
					Nil	4

It is sometimes claimed that the IRR is not a realistic measure of return because the method implies that a project's annual cash flows must be capable of being reinvested to earn the project's IRR. In the case of projects with high IRRs – say, 20% – such high returns are not available in the capital markets without very high risk, so it is argued that the IRR is invalid.

This *reinvestment assumption* corresponds with the concept of the IRR as the compound rate that results in a nil NTV. This assumes that each year's cash flow is compounded at the IRR rate to the end of the project. However, the example in Table 4.2 shows that such an assumption is not inherent to the IRR. Project A actually earns the investor 13.16% per annum on his capital invested before it is repaid. The IRR is a valid measure of return. However, it should be appreciated that the IRR is not necessarily a percentage return on all capital invested over the whole life of the project. It is a return on capital until the capital is repaid by cash inflows. As Table 4.2 illustrates, in the case of Project A only £35.35 earns 13.16% per annum over the full four years.

Apart from the disadvantage that the IRR for multi-period projects cannot be solved by a simple algebraic equation, the method has a number of other potential pitfalls. We shall go on to look at these next.

MULTIPLE POSITIVE SOLUTIONS (ROOTS)

In Chapter 3, we used the iterative method to obtain one solution for a project's IRR. In fact, because of the nature of the mathematical equation, there can be a number of mathematically correct solutions (positive or negative) to the IRR, but only one that is economically valid. The solution obtained may be mathematically correct, but economically invalid. In project appraisal, it is essential to identify the economically valid IRR. In this section, we shall learn how to identify projects where a problem might arise, then look at ways in which the problem might be avoided.

Identifying Cases with Multiple Positive Solutions

Projects A and B are said to have conventional cash flows; that is, where an initial cash outflow is followed by a series of cash inflows. In such cases, where the sum of positive cash flows exceeds the sum of negative cash flows, the economically valid IRR must be positive, and any negative solutions to the IRR can be ignored as being invalid. We must, however, identify cases where there may be more than one positive solution.

It is possible for there to be as many positive solutions to the IRR as there are changes in the sign of the cash flow (Descartes' change of sign rule). We shall explore this possibility using the cash flows shown in Table 4.3. In the

Table 4.3 Projects C, D, E

	Expected cash flows (£) *Year*				
	0	*1*	*2*	*3*	*4*
Project C	–100	+50	+50	+50	+50
Project D	-50	-50	+50	+50	+50
Project E	–100	+50	+50	+50	-10

table, Project C contains only one change of sign in the cash flow. It changes from negative in Year 0 to positive in Year 1, and remains positive thereafter. No problem of multiple positive solutions can occur in such a situation.

Project D has only one change of sign in the cash flow (between Years 1 and 2), so again, there will only be one positive solution. However, for Project E, there are two changes in the sign of the cash flow, from Year 0 to Year 1, and from Year 3 to Year 4. This means that there may be two positive solutions to the IRR.

Multiple positive solutions will only occur in cases of *negative capital outlay*. These are cases that have a point in the cash flow prior to a second or subsequent sign change to a negative cash flow, at which the previous negative cash flow has been more than repaid. (At that point, a positive IRR has been earned.) Project E is an example of such a case. Prior to Year 4, the previous outlay of £100 has been more than repaid by the incoming cash flows in Years 1, 2 and 3 (which total £150). In this situation, there *will* be more than one positive solution to the IRR.

Adjusting Cases with Multiple Positive Solutions

The simplest way of dealing with the problem of multiple positive roots is to derive an amended cash flow of equivalent value (to the investor) to the original, but from which the second (or subsequent) change in sign has been eradicated. We can do this for Project E by discounting Year 4's negative cash flow into Year 3 (using the investor's required rate of return), and deducting that discounted negative figure from Year 3's positive cash flow to get an adjusted (positive) net figure. The negative cash flow is amortised.

If we assume that the investor's required return is 15%, then the equivalent value in Year 3 of –£10 in Year 4 is:

$$-£10 \times \frac{1}{(1 + 0.15)} = -£8.70$$

So, we subtract £8.70 from the £50 cash flow in Year 3 to get the adjusted figure of £41.30. This method produces a cash flow of equivalent value to the original, and the IRR of the adjusted cash flow is then calculated in the normal way. If the positive cash flow in Year 3 had not been sufficient to absorb the discounted Year 4 negative cash flow, the net Year 3 figure would have been discounted into Year 2 and amortised. This process is sometimes called the *extended IRR method*.

For Project E, the IRR of the adjusted cash flow is 20.2% (see Table 4.4). This is marginally below the true IRR for the unadjusted cash flow (20.3%) because the 15% discount rate applied to the Year 4 cash flow is below the IRR of the project as a whole. The adjustment under-discounts the Year 4 cash flow into Year 3.

Table 4.4 Project E

Year	*Adjusted cash flow (£)*	*Discount factor @ 20.2%*	*Discounted cash flow (£)*
0	−100	1.000	−100.00
1	+50	0.832	+41.60
2	+50	0.692	+34.60
3	+41.30	0.576	+23.80
			NPV @ 20.2% = 0

MUTUALLY EXCLUSIVE PROJECTS

Care should be taken when using the IRR method to identify the most profitable of a number of mutually exclusive projects. For example, a real estate developer may have a number of alternative schemes in mind for a single city centre site, but can only undertake one project on the site, and proceeding with one project would exclude the others.

The IRR method can be unreliable if the *duration* of alternative projects is different. It would select a project earning 20% per annum for five years in preference to one earning 19% per annum for twenty years. The IRR method can also select the wrong project if the *capital costs or cash flow profiles* of alternative projects are significantly different (for example, where one project earns high initial returns and low later returns, and the alternative project earns low initial returns but high later returns).

Consider the example of Projects F and G in Table 4.5, having different capital costs. The required return in each case is 15%. Project F produces the higher NPV, while Project G produces the higher IRR. The two decision criteria give conflicting signals. The conflict arises because the NPV and IRR measure different things. The NPV is the present value of the expected cash flow measured in pounds. The IRR is a measure of the percentage return on capital invested. The IRR method would select an investment providing a 25% return on £100 in preference to an investment giving a 24% return on £1 million. This would make little sense if the two investments were mutually exclusive (and the investor had £1m to invest, and the smaller investment could not be repeated): the investor would make more profit by taking on the £1m project.

For mutually exclusive projects where the capital costs or cash flow profiles differ substantially, the IRR method is not reliable. However, the method can be adapted for these situations to select the same project as the NPV. The adaptation is known as the *incremental IRR method*. This has various applications to real-estate appraisal, which are investigated later in the book.

The incremental IRR method involves calculating the IRR of the difference between the cash flows of the two projects, known as the incremental cash flow. If the IRR of the incremental cash flow exceeds the investor's required return, the larger of the two projects should be selected. This is because the (notional) incremental project is profitable, and the only way to take on the incremental project is to take on the larger project. Conversely, if the IRR of the incremental cash flow is below the required return, the smaller project should be selected.

To illustrate this, we shall apply the incremental IRR method to Projects F and G, as shown in Table 4.6. In this example, the incremental cash flow

Table 4.5 Projects F and G

	Expected cash flows (£) Year				*IRR p.a. (%)*	*NPV @ 15% (£)*
	0	*1*	*2*	*3*		
Project F	−100	+50	+50	+50	23.4	14.2
Project G	−40	+22	+22	+22	29.9	10.2

Table 4.6 Incremental IRR method

	Expected cash flows (£) *Year*				*IRR (%)*
	0	*1*	*2*	*3*	
Project F	−100	+50	+50	+50	
Project G	−40	+22	+22	+22	
F – G	−60	+28	+28	+28	18.9

(F – G) produces an IRR of 18.9%. This exceeds the investor's required return of 15%, which means that we should select the larger project, Project F. In its incremental form, the IRR will choose the same projects as the NPV method.

THE IRR METHOD AND RISK

The return required by investors from a project will reflect their perception of the project's risk. When using the NPV (or NTV) method, it is valid to select the project with the highest NPV (NTV), because the project's risk has been reflected in the discount rate (or compound rate) used. The NPV is risk-adjusted.

However, it is not necessarily valid to select the project with the highest expected IRR. The IRR is a measure of percentage return on capital, which has not taken into account the cost of the capital or the project's risk. When applying the IRR method, the expected IRR should be compared with the required IRR, where the required IRR has been chosen to reflect the risk of the project. The project selected by this method will generally be the one in which the expected IRR exceeds the required IRR by the greatest margin.

RETURN ON CAPITAL OR COST OF CAPITAL?

We have looked at examples in which the IRR measures the *return* on capital invested. However, the IRR may also measure the *cost* of capital; for example, the cost of capital raised by sale and leaseback (see Chapter 9), or the cost of capital raised by borrowing.

Consider cash flows H and J in Table 4.7. Cash flow H is a conventional investment, where £100 is invested to earn £10 per annum in years 1–4 plus the return of capital at the end of Year 4. Cash flow J arises from £100 being borrowed (Year 0) at a 10% per annum interest rate, with capital being repaid at the end of Year 4.

The cash flows are the same, but the signs are reversed, yet the IRR in each case is +10%. In the case of H, the IRR is a return on capital invested, but in J the IRR measures the cost of the capital borrowed. The IRR does not distinguish between the two, but merely measures the relationship between the negative and positive cash flows in each case.

The IRR is sometimes criticised as a decision criterion because it does not distinguish between return on capital invested and cost of capital raised. Confusion can result in the case of complex cash flows with a number of sign changes. However, in the context of property investment, it will normally be obvious what is being measured. None the less, the appraiser needs to be alive to such idiosyncrasies of the IRR.

Table 4.7 Cash flows H and J

	Expected cash flows (£) Year					*IRR p.a. (%)*
	0	*1*	*2*	*3*	*4*	
Cash flow H	−100	+10	+10	+10	+110	+10
Cash flow J	+100	−10	−10	−10	−110	+10

APPRAISAL METHODS – SUMMARY OF RELATIVE MERITS

Over the last three chapters, we have looked at five different investment appraisal methods:

- Payback Period;
- Average Return;
- net present value (NPV);
- net terminal value (NTV); and
- internal rate of return (IRR).

We have assumed that the ultimate objective of the decision-maker is to maximise the investor's wealth. In pursuit of that aim, the Payback Period and Average Return are unreliable as decision criteria because they fail to take properly into account the amount and timing of all cash flows to be generated by investments. In contrast, NPV, NTV and IRR methods are all consistent with the objective of maximising investors' wealth. In fact, the NPV measures the value added as a result of taking on an investment. In the case of a company taking on a project with an NPV of £1m, the company's net asset value should be raised by £1m immediately the decision to take on the project has been made, and should be reflected in a corresponding rise in the price of the company's shares.

The NPV and NTV methods value the financial surplus to be generated by an investment over and above the repayment of capital invested and the investor's required return on that capital. Both criteria measure what an economist would call 'super-normal profit'; that is, a profit over and above that needed to persuade the investor to take on the investment.

The NPV (and NTV) calculations are conceptually and mathematically sound. If the correct discount (compound) rate is used, these methods will always indicate the economically correct decision. However, the discount (compound) rate must reflect risk, and risk is virtually impossible to assess accurately. A wrong assessment of risk can result in a wrong decision whatever the appraisal method used.

Essentially, the IRR measures the relationship between an investment's cash inflows and outflows. Hence, it can measure either the return on capital invested or the cost of capital raised. When measuring a return on capital, the IRR is a rate of return earned by the investment over and above the repayment of the capital. However, there are a number of problems associated with its application:

- When measuring the return from a project, the IRR does not take into account risk or the cost of capital, so investment decisions using the IRR method need to be made by a comparison between the expected IRR and the IRR required from the capital invested in the project;
- The expected IRR is more difficult to calculate manually than either the NPV or NTV, although the operation can be carried out quickly and simply using a suitable calculator or computer software;
- Cash flows may need to be adjusted to eliminate cases with multiple positive roots;
- The IRR can indicate the wrong decision in the case of mutually exclusive projects;
- In complex cases, confusion can arise over whether the IRR measures a return on capital or a cost of capital.

An investment's expected IRR is the expected *average* return per annum over the life of the investment, and should be compared with a required IRR, which reflects the investment's overall risk and cost of capital. However, different parts or stages of a project may incur different levels of risk, and the cost of capital might be expected to change at some future period during a project. With the NPV (and NTV) methods, these factors can be allowed for by changing the discount (compound) rate applied to the cash flows of different elements of the project (see Chapter 5, SAQ 5.3). In this respect, the NPV and NTV methods are more flexible than the IRR.

On the other hand, the NPV lacks a sense of proportion – a project's NPV is not related to the scale of the project. An NPV of £1m is good if derived from a project costing £4m. However, an NPV of £1m is not so good if the project costs £100m, because a small change in cost or revenue could wipe it out. Therefore, in comparison with the rather mechanistic nature of the NPV and NTV decision criteria, the IRR method is more judgemental. The decision-maker makes the judgement to select a project or not after weighing up the difference between the required and expected IRRs, in the knowledge that risk is unavoidable and that it is impossible to be specific about the required rate of return.

It may be for this reason that the IRR method seems to be more popular with decision-makers in industry, whereas academics and authors of textbooks frequently prefer the NPV, sometimes to the exclusion of the IRR. However, the argument about which is the better method is irrelevant: both should be used simultaneously, and decision-makers should become familiar with both methods. Each has its advantages and disadvantages, and each can be ascertained quickly using a calculator. If the methods indicate different decisions, then the reasons should be investigated and the methods reconciled.

The potential pitfalls of the IRR method are not a sufficient reason to discard that option; in fact, understanding these pitfalls is important to an overall understanding of DCF techniques. The IRR is used widely in the property industry as well as in the world of finance and investment generally. It is much too important a tool to exclude in favour of the NPV. In fact, arguably, the NPV, NTV and IRR should not be considered as different methods, but as different perspectives on the same method. Ultimately, investment decisions depend on judgements, not calculations. Appraisal techniques are aids to making sound judgements, but should not be applied in a mechanistic way.

SUMMARY

This chapter has:

- investigated in further depth the complex nature of the IRR and its idiosyncrasies;

- identified the circumstances in which particular care is needed in applying the IRR method;
- introduced the extended IRR and incremental IRR methods; and
- ended with a discussion of the relative characteristics and merits of the IRR and NPV methods.

The chapter has introduced a number of quite difficult issues which may seem indigestible in the text, but I hope clearer and simpler when applied in examples. The reader is particularly recommended to attempt and work through the questions attached to this chapter in order to consolidate an understanding of the concepts.

SELF-ASSESSMENT QUESTIONS

4.1 What is an IRR?

4.2 Estimate the IRR percentage per annum of the cash flows shown in Table 4.8. Calculations are not required. Assume that all cash flows are made at the end of the year.

4.3 Refer again to Table 4.8. Which cash flow has the higher NPV: Cash Flow 4 or 5?

Table 4.8 Estimating the IRR

	Cash flows (£)				
	Year				
	0	*1*	*2*	*3*	*4*
1	–100	+10	+10	+10	+10 p.a. into perpetuity
2	–100	+10	+10	+10	+10 p.a. until year 14
3	–100	+10	+10	+10	+10
4	–100	+101	–	–	–
5	–100	+1	+101	–	–
6	–	+100	–1	–1	–101
7	–100	+25	+25	+25	+25
8	–100	+26	+26	+26	+26
9	–100	–	–	–	+104
10	–50	–50	+101	–	–
11	–200	+220	–	–	–
12	–100	–10	–10	–	–

4.4 In the case of a conventional cash flow, outline the checks you should make to test for the existence of multiple positive solutions to the IRR.

4.5 In which of the cash flows in Table 4.9 does the problem of multiple positive solutions arise in calculating the IRR?

4.6 Calculate the extended IRR of Cash Flow E in Table 4.9, assuming the investor's required return on the project is 15%.

4.7 Examine the cash flows, NPVs and IRRs for Projects V and W in Table 4.10, and provide three reasons that could explain why the IRR criterion is signalling the wrong project selection. Assume that the target IRR is 15% in both cases, and that the projects are mutually exclusive.

4.8 Projects X, Y and Z are similar in terms of cost, duration and cash flow profile, but different in the level of risk involved. Appraisal has

Table 4.9 Checking for multiple positive roots

	Cash flows (£) Year					
	0	*1*	*2*	*3*	*4*	*5*
A	–600	+200	+200	+200	+200	+200
B	–200	–300	–400	+500	+600	+700
C	–400	+100	+500	+100	–100	–200
D	–100	–200	–400	+600	–200	+800
E	–500	–200	+200	+600	+200	–100
F	+900	–100	–100	–200	–300	–400

Table 4.10 Projects V and W

	Expected cash flows (£) Year						*NPV @ 15% (£)*	*Expected IRR p.a. (%)*
	0	*1*	*2*	*3*	*4*	*5*		
Project V	–400	+300	+200	+100	–	–	77.8	28.9
Project W	–700	+100	+200	+300	+400	+500	212.7	24.4

Table 4.11 Projects X, Y and Z

	Expected IRR (%)	*Required IRR (%)*
Project X	20	15
Project Y	18	12
Project Z	12	10

Table 4.12 Projects M and N

	Expected cash flows (£) Year					*IRR p.a. (%)*
	0	*1*	*2*	*3*	*4*	
Project M	–350	+130	+130	+130	+130	18
Project N	–200	+90	+80	+70	+60	20

produced the expected IRRs and required IRRs shown in Table 4.11, with the different required IRRs reflecting the different risks of the projects. Assuming the projects are mutually exclusive, which would you select using the IRR criterion?

4.9 Using the IRR method, you have to select either Project M or Project N, which are expected to produce the cash flows shown in Table 4.12. Calculation of the projects' IRRs indicates Project N to be the more profitable, but given the different capital costs of the two projects, you wish to check the decision using the incremental IRR method. Calculate the incremental IRR in this case, and explain which project to select. Assume that the risk of the two projects is similar, and that the required return is 12% in each case.

ANSWERS TO SELF-ASSESSMENT QUESTIONS

4.1 A simple answer is that the IRR is the percentage rate that, when used to discount a project's cash flow, results in a nil NPV.

A better understanding of the concept is given by the definition of the IRR as the rate of return earned on the capital invested in a project before that capital is repaid. It is a rate of return earned per period, averaged over the life of the investment, which takes into account the timing of cash flows.

That is true for a conventional investment, but where a cash flow represents payments made for capital raised, the IRR measures the cost of the capital per period (prior to the repayment or amortisation of the capital raised).

4.2 The IRRs of these cash flows are best understood by the concept of the IRR as the rate of return earned per annum on the capital invested before it is repaid (see Table 4.8).

Cash Flow 1
In this case, the capital is never repaid, but 10% per annum is earned for ever. So, the IRR is 10% per annum.

Cash Flow 2
Here, £10 per annum is earned for a period of 14 years. The total income (£140) exceeds the capital outflow in Year 0, so the IRR must be positive, but clearly less than in Cash Flow 1. In fact, the IRR is 4.8% per annum. You could not estimate that accurately, but you should have expected a positive, single-figure IRR.

Cash Flow 3
Here, £10 per annum is earned for four years only. In this case, the incoming cash flow (£40) does not even repay the initial capital outflow (£100), so the IRR is strongly negative. The precise figure is –28.7% per annum.

Cash Flow 4
Here, the incoming cash flow in Year 1 is sufficient to repay all outstanding capital and earn 1% over and above that repayment. Hence, the IRR is 1%.

Cash Flow 5
Imagine that the £100 capital invested is repaid out of the £101 earned in Year 2. Prior to that, 1% is earned in each of the two years. So, the IRR is 1% per annum.

Cash Flow 6
Again, the IRR per annum is 1%, for essentially the same reasons as in Cash Flow 5. However, in this case, the IRR measures a cost of capital raised, rather than a return on capital invested. The cash flow could represent £100 being borrowed in Year 1, and 1% interest being paid annually prior to repayment of the debt in Year 4.

Cash Flow 7
The sum of the incoming cash exactly equals the initial capital outlay. So, the IRR is exactly nil. The capital invested is repaid, but there is no return on that capital.

Cash Flow 8
At first glance, this might look like an IRR of 1% per annum, because £1 is earned each year over and above the repayment of capital. But the IRR of the following cash flow is 1%:

−100 + 1 + 1 + 1 + 101.

Cash Flow 8 produces the same total inflow but, on average, much earlier. Much of the £100 invested is repaid in the early years, so there is less capital outstanding in later years compared with the above. If £25 of each cash flow in Years 1 and 2 was used to repay capital, only £50 would be outstanding at the start of Year 3. Therefore, the £1 surplus in Year 3 would earn a 2% return in that year. So, the IRR of the cash flow is greater than 1%. In fact, it is 1.6% per annum.

Cash Flow 9
Here again, the total inflow is £104 over the four years, but because it is all received in the last year, the IRR must be less than 1% per annum. It is in fact 0.99% per annum.

Cash Flow 10
Again, the IRR in this case is less than 1% per annum because the £50 paid out in Year 0 is outstanding over two years before being repaid. The IRR is 0.67% per annum.

Cash Flow 11
The IRR is 10%, because after repaying the £200 outstanding, the remaining £20 received in Year 1 is 10% of the capital invested.

Cash Flow 12
There is no IRR in this case, because there is no incoming cash flow to relate to the outgoing cash flows.

On page 43 it was explained that the IRR per annum of a cash flow is not necessarily earned on *all* the capital initially invested over the *full* life of the project. This is the case in Cash Flows 2 and 8. In these cases, part of the cash flow in each year repays some of the capital invested before the last year of the project. But, for example, in Cash Flows 4, 5, 6, 9, 10 and 11, no capital is repaid until the final year. The IRR is earned on all capital invested over the full life of these projects.

4.3 It depends on the discount rate. At a discount rate of 1%, the two cash flows each have a nil NPV. At any discount rate above 1%, both NPVs are negative, with that of Cash Flow 4 being the least negative (that is, closer to nil NPV).

4.4 (1) Check whether the sum of the positive cash flow exceeds the sum of the negative cash flow. If so, the economically correct IRR must be positive.
(2) Check the number of sign changes in the cash flow. If there is only one sign change, there can only be one positive solution to the IRR.
(3) If there is more than one sign change, check for negative capital outlay; that is, check whether, at any point in the cash flow prior to a second or subsequent change in sign (to a negative cash flow), the sum of all previous negative cash flows has been repaid and more by incoming cash flows. If negative capital exists, you need to calculate an extended IRR.

4.5 *Cash Flow A*
Incoming cash flows substantially exceed the initial outgoing cash flow, and there is only one change in sign. So, the IRR is clearly positive (19.86% per annum) and there can be no problem of multiple positive roots.

Cash Flow B
Here, again, there is only one change in the sign of the cash flow, and the total of incoming cash flows is double the total outgoing cash flows. So, the IRR must be unique and strongly positive. It is 27.15% per annum.

Cash Flow C
Here, there are two changes in the sign of the cash flow, signalling the possibility of the problem of multiple positive roots. However, the sum of the incoming cash flows exactly equals the sum of the outgoing cash flows, so the economically valid IRR is exactly nil.

Cash Flow D
In this case, the sum of the incoming cash flows exceeds the sum of the outgoing cash flows, so the IRR must be positive. There are three changes in the sign of the cash flow. However, the problem of multiple positive roots will not occur, because the condition of negative capital outlay does not exist. The £600 in Year 3 is not sufficient to repay previous negative cash flows. The IRR is 22.30%.

Cash Flow E
The IRR in this case must be positive, because the sum of incoming

cash exceeds the sum of outgoing cash. However, there are two changes in the sign of the cash flow, and negative capital outlay (at some positive IRR) will occur after Years 3 and 4. An IRR of 10.56% is calculated, but this is unreliable as it may be an economically invalid solution (see Question 4.6).

Cash Flow F
Previous cash flows have featured projects where capital has initially been expended to earn subsequent returns. This is the opposite: £900 is being raised at the cost of a future negative cash flow.

Although the sum of the negative cash flow exceeds the positive, the IRR is positive, but it is measuring the cost of capital, not a return on capital. The IRR is 5.60%. There can be no problem of multiple positive solutions, because there is only one sign change in the cash flow.

4.6 The potential for multiple positive roots arises because of the second change in the sign of the cash flow. So, the problem can be avoided by discounting the –£100 in Year 5 and deducting that from the positive cash flow in Year 4.

The equivalent value in Year 4 of the –£100 in Year 5 is:

$$-100 \times \frac{1}{(1 + 0.15)} = -£86.96.$$

The adjusted cash flow is as shown in Table 4.13. The extended IRR of this cash flow, worked out using a calculator, is 10.71% per annum. This is close to the IRR of 10.56% calculated from the unadjusted cash flow, suggesting that this was correct. The extended IRR will be somewhat higher, because discounting the Year 5 negative cash flow at 15% is reducing its value relative to the reduction in value implied by the 10.56% rate.

Table 4.13 Project E, adjusted cash flow

Cash flow (£) *Years*				
0	*1*	*2*	*3*	*4*
-500	-200	+200	+600	+200 -86.96
-500	-200	+200	+600	+113.04

4.7 If 15% is the correct discount rate, the NPV method has correctly selected Project W in preference to Project V. Three reasons why the IRR criterion might select the wrong project in this case are:

- the different initial costs of the projects;
- the different cash flow profiles – Project V produces relatively high early returns, while Project W produces high late returns; and
- the different durations of the projects.

The source of the error is that the IRR is merely a percentage return on capital per period, not a measure of capital profit. It implies that a high percentage return per annum on a small amount of capital invested for a short period is preferable to a lower percentage return on a larger amount of money for a longer period.

4.8 Project Y should be selected, because the margin between the expected and target IRR is the greatest. It would be wrong to select Project X just because it has the highest expected return.

4.9 The incremental cash flow is calculated and discounted at a first trial rate of 15%, see Table 4.14. As the NPV of the incremental cash flow is positive at a 15% discount rate, we know that the incremental IRR exceeds 15%. It is not necessary to calculate the incremental IRR more accurately. As the incremental IRR exceeds the required IRR of 12%, the larger project, Project M, should be selected. Calculation of the NPVs of the two projects using a 12% discount rate confirms Project M as the preferred project.

Table 4.14 Incremental IRR, Projects M and N

Year	*Project M (£)*	*Project N (£)*	*Incremental cash flow (£)*	*Discount factor @ 15%*	*Discounted cash flow (£)*
0	–350	–200	–150	1.000	–150.00
1	+130	+90	+40	0.870	34.80
2	+130	+80	+50	0.756	37.80
3	+130	+70	+60	0.658	39.48
4	+130	+60	+70	0.572	40.00
				NPV @ 15% =	+2.12

5

Key Principles for DCF Practice

OVERVIEW

So far, we have merely examined the basic concepts and techniques of discounted cash-flow (DCF) analysis. Its practical application to investment decision-making requires careful estimation of expected cash flows and required returns. But these estimates need to be based on a set of rules and principles. This chapter examines various important issues in DCF appraisal, and identifies the rules and principles that determine good practice.

A PERSPECTIVE FOR DCF APPRAISAL

This book examines cash-flow appraisal as an aid to investment decision-making, primarily in a private-sector context, where the investor might be an individual, company or investing institution. A basic assumption made already is that the objective of appraisal is to assist the investor to select investments that maximise wealth.

Wealth maximisation implies that investors should select investments according to the risk *they* will face and the returns *they* will receive, net of all expenses, including taxation. Therefore, all such costs need to be taken into account in the appraisal. But different investors pay tax at different rates; indeed, some are exempt, which highlights the need to undertake the appraisal from the *perspective of the investor* in question. That means, for example, that cash flows should be based on the investor's taxation liability, and the required return based on the investor's cost of capital and risk exposure.

CAPITAL RATIONING AND PROJECT INDEPENDENCE ISSUES

Capital Rationing

So far, it has been implied that a profit-maximising investor should undertake all projects for which:

- the NPV or NTV is nil or greater than nil; and
- the expected IRR equals or exceeds the target IRR.

However, in reality, the funds and management resources available to an individual investor are limited. Thus, frequently, the investor must choose one or more projects out of a number of alternatives. In this situation, the rule is to select that group of projects that will provide the highest aggregate NPV with the capital available. NPVs are additive. The IRR method is not suitable for solving capital rationing problems, essentially because it is a measure of percentage return on capital, and not a measure of expected profit.

Different projects have different capital costs, so projects should be ranked on the basis of NPV per £ sterling of capital cost; that is, the *benefit/cost* ratio. Projects should be chosen on the basis of this ratio until all the capital available has been used up. We shall illustrate this process by the following example.

A property developer has undertaken detailed appraisals of the costs and income expected from six potential developments, A to F, all of which are to be sold on completion. Table 5.1 shows the expected net cash flow and NPV for each of the projects, assuming a target return of 15% per annum (all are assumed to be of similar risk).

Table 5.1 Projects A–F

	Cash flows (£)				*NPV*	*Benefit/*	*Rank*
	Year				*@ 15%*	*cost ratio*	
	0	*1*	*2*	*3*	*(£)*		
Project A	−160	+20	−150	+450	39.9	+0.25	3
Project B	−120	−80	+280	–	22.2	+0.18	5
Project C	−210	−100	+450	–	43.3	+0.21	4
Project D	−100	−100	−200	+600	56.3	+0.56	2
Project E	−100	−150	−250	+750	73.7	+0.74	1
Project F	−100	−100	+240	–	−5.5	−0.05	6

If no capital scarcity existed, a wealth-maximising developer would undertake all the projects except Project F, which has a negative NPV and is unprofitable. However, we shall assume that this developer's parent company has imposed a maximum capital expenditure of £500 in Year 0. Good financial management requires a company to plan ahead for its capital requirements. Our developer has profitable opportunities amounting to £690 in Year 0, but is limited to a maximum expenditure of £500. Which projects should be chosen?

The developer must identify the combination of projects having a total cost in Year 0 not exceeding £500, that will provide the highest NPV. This is done by dividing each project's NPV by its Year 0 cost to find the Year 0 benefit/cost ratio, ranking the projects according to their benefit/cost ratios, then selecting projects successively according to their ranking until all the capital has been used up. Therefore, in this example, the total NPV would be maximised by selecting successively projects E, D and A, plus two thirds of C, to give:

$$\begin{aligned} \text{Total NPV} &= £73.7 + £56.3 + £39.9 + 2/3\,(£43.3) \\ &= £198.8 \end{aligned}$$

The selection assumes that Project C is *divisible*: that it is practicable to undertake two-thirds of it rather than the whole. Some property development projects are divisible; for example, housing developments on greenfield sites may benefit from being phased over a number of years. In other circumstances – for example, a city centre office or retail development – divisibility is not practicable. In that situation, simple ranking of projects by benefit/cost ratio is unreliable. The aim instead is to identify the combination of whole projects that maximises total NPV while keeping within the cost limit. This requires a trial-and-error examination of all possible combinations. Assuming indivisibility in the example above, three possible combinations for the options considered in Table 5.1 are shown below:

Try: E + D + A + B	NPV = 73.7 + 56.3 + 39.9 + 22.2 = £192.1
Try: E + D + C	NPV = 73.7 + 56.3 + 43.3 = £173.3
Try: E +A + C	NPV = 73.7 + 39.9 + 43.3 = £156.9

Other combinations are possible, but it is clear that the combination of E, D, A and B maximises total NPV for whole projects.

Project Independence

Until now, we have assumed implicitly that all projects in Table 5.1 are independent. But this may not be the case. For example, two or more projects might be mutually exclusive or interdependent. Examples of mutually-exclusive projects might include:

- two alternative developments for the same site; or
- two shopping developments within close proximity, where there is sufficient demand to sustain only one.

Where projects are interdependent, the viability of one depends on the other. For example, where Project A is a shopping development, its profitability might be dependent on Project B, a major housing project nearby.

In these situations, the optimal solution can be found by proceeding through all possible combinations on a trial and error basis, helped by the benefit/cost ratios. For example, we shall now assume that Projects D and E, from Table 5.1, are mutually exclusive, E being a more elaborate development of the same site. We shall also assume that we are seeking the optimal combination of whole projects within the £500 Year 0 limit. As D and E have the same Year 0 cost, but E has the higher NPV, then D would be excluded and the optimal group of projects would be E + A + C, as shown in Table 5.2.

Table 5.2 Most profitable group of developments

Project	*B/C rank*	*Outlay (£)*	*NPV (£)*
E	1	100	73.7
A	3	160	39.9
C	4	210	43.3
Totals		470	156.9

Now assume that only Projects B and C are mutually exclusive. As these have different Year 0 costs, we have to examine the alternatives under the two scenarios, once with B excluded and once with C excluded. First, we identify the two total NPVs with Project B excluded:

Try: E + D + A   NPV = 73.7 + 56.3 + 39.9 = 169.9
Try: E + C + A   NPV = 73.7 + 43.3 + 39.9 = 156.9

Next, we find the NPV with Project C excluded:

Try: E + D + A + B   NPV = 73.7 + 56.3 + 39.9 + 22.2 = 192.1

Therefore, although Project C has a superior NPV and benefit/cost ratio to Project B, it would be excluded in favour of Project B (together with E, D and A) because B's lower Year 0 cost allows a more profitable combination of projects within the £500 constraint.

These examples of capital rationing and project independence illustrate important concepts of significance to practical investment decision-making. But the cases considered have been restricted to *single period* capital rationing – Year 0 in our examples. In reality, constraints may extend over a number of future periods. *Multi-period* capital rationing creates a more complex problem, requiring linear programming techniques for its solution, but this is beyond the scope of this book.

THE RELATIONSHIP BETWEEN CASH FLOWS AND THE REQUIRED RETURN

The essential rationale of DCF appraisal is twofold:

- if the amount and timing of all income and expenditure that will result from an investment decision is traced, this provides all that is necessary to know in order to calculate the investment's return; and
- if this return exceeds the investor's cost of capital plus an allowance for risk, illiquidity and so on, then the investment will add to the investor's wealth.

Therefore, cash-flow appraisal is essentially a comparison between the *return required* from an investment and the *return* it is *expected* to provide. This is most obvious with the IRR method, where decisions are based on a comparison between the required IRR and the expected IRR. However, the concept is equally applicable to the NPV method (where expected cash flows are discounted at the investor's required IRR) and to the NTV. In all three methods, the analysis is a comparison between an expected return and a required return.

In estimating the cash flows and required return, a good general rule is that expected returns should be reflected in the cash flows and required returns in the required IRR. In this case, cash flows should be best estimates of the amount and timing of all income and expenditure expected to arise *as a result of* taking on the investment. The required return should be the minimum return acceptable; that is, the return just sufficient to persuade the investor to take on the investment. It should reflect such issues as the cost of the capital invested, and the investment's risk and liquidity. In the case of projects, as distinct from existing portfolio investments, the required return should also include a return for enterprise.

However, practice varies from the above norm, and a defining principle of cash-flow appraisal is that the cash flows must be *mutually consistent* with the required return. For example, a simple rule of thumb sometimes used by property developers to assess their required return on a project is to double their cost of capital. So, if the developer's cost of capital is 8% per annum, the target return might be 16% per annum; the extra 8% to reflect the profit required for the developer's enterprise and to compensate for the project's risk and the illiquidity of capital invested.

Alternatively, property developers often feel more confident in assessing the required return for enterprise and risk as a capital profit, estimated by reference to the project's total cost (say, 15% of cost). In this case, the project would be appraised appropriately by entering that required profit as a negative cash flow at the end of the project and discounting the project's cash flow at the 8% cost of capital rate. If the cash flow has been compiled net of the return required for enterprise and risk, the discount rate must be determined similarly.

Either practice is legitimate; in fact, if the 8% yield premium in the former case was consistent with the profit take-out in the latter, the NPV outcome would be the same. The crucial point is that the cash flow must be consistent with the required return. If the developer's required profit was represented in both the cash flow and the target return, there would be double counting and the appraisal would be invalid.

Another example of mutual consistency is provided by the use of *certainty equivalents* in cash flow appraisal. Making appropriate allowance for risk probably poses the single greatest challenge in investment appraisal. Conventionally, using the NPV method, risk is reflected in the discount rate, and cash flows are best estimates of actual income and expenditure. However, a technique sometimes used is to convert expected cash flows into certainty equivalents. These are no-risk cash flows judged to be equivalent in value to the risky best estimates. By converting best-estimate cash flows into (lower) no-risk equivalents, risk has been allowed for in the cash flows. Hence, to be consistent, the discount rate must be a risk-free rate. As long as the adjustments are consistent, the lower cash flows and lower discount rate should result in the same NPV as calculated by the conventional method.

Certainty equivalence has been introduced here for illustrative purposes, but the technique is not used in this book.

ALLOWING FOR THE COST OF DEBT

Compatibility between expected and required returns is a particular issue when appraising investments that are part-financed by debt. An investment can be appraised, either:

- by comparing its expected return with the investor's required return on capital invested (debt and equity); or
- by comparing the expected return on the equity capital alone with the required return on equity.

In the latter case, the expected IRR on the equity is calculated after deducting the cash flows attributable to the debt capital financing the investment (see Tables 1.2 and 1.3 in Chapter 1). This procedure commonly is adopted for appraising real estate investments in the USA, and seems rational, because property is often purchased with mortgage debt secured on the investment being acquired. The investment and its financing are considered to be inseparable.

However, if this process is adopted, the expected IRR calculated is the expected return on the *equity capital* invested, and not the investment itself. The required IRR must be consistent with that, but because the return to equity in this case is a risky geared residual, the required risk premium will tend to be high and difficult to assess accurately. In fact, as we saw in Chapter 1 (Table 1.1), the risk to equity depends on the *level* of gearing. The higher the gearing, the higher the risk. The problem of quantifying this risk and reflecting it appropriately in the required return is one reason to reject the system of incorporating debt cash flows into the calculation of the expected return. Another, more fundamental, reason is explained in Chapter 7, where we examine the subject in more detail.

The system illustrated in Tables 1.2 and 1.3 is useful to test the impact of different rental or capital growth scenarios. However, for formal DCF appraisal, the practice recommended here is to reflect the investor's overall cost of capital (debt and equity) in the required return, and *not* to incorporate debt capital or interest payments in the cash flow.

SUNK COSTS AND OPPORTUNITY COSTS

The general rule in estimating cash flows is that these should be best estimates of the amount and timing of all income and expenditure expected to arise *as a result of* taking on the investment (excluding cash flows arising from its *funding*). Only cash flows affected by the decision should be included. Therefore, 'sunk costs' should be excluded. These are costs related to the investment but unaffected by the decision to invest. Examples include the cost of an appraisal carried out in order to arrive at the decision whether or not to invest, and the cost of an *option* to purchase land for development. If such costs do not arise *as a result of* the decision to invest (that is, they are unaffected by the decision), then they are economically irrelevant to the decision and should be excluded from the appraisal.

Similarly, an income that apparently is associated with an investment should be excluded from the appraisal if it would be receivable despite the decision.

Another important principle in DCF analysis is that where a direct cost differs from the opportunity cost, the latter should be used. This introduces an exception to the general rule that cash flows should only include actual income and expenditure arising as a result of the decision to invest, but emphasises the rational economic nature of DCF appraisal. To illustrate, assume that a property developer is appraising a potential development project using a site bought several years before for £10m. If the development proceeds, no actual cash flow will arise that represents the cost of the site, but clearly the site has an economic cost (opportunity cost) which must be included in the appraisal. Opportunity cost is the value forgone as a result of a decision. So, if the project proceeds, the developer will have forgone the benefit that he or she could have gained from alternatives such as using the site for a different project or selling it on the market. The opportunity cost is the highest of such alternative values.

If, in this case, the developer envisages no alternative profitable development and the current value of the site is now £15m (net of any taxes or expenses of sale), that would be its opportunity cost. If its current value is £5m (net), that would be its opportunity cost. The £10m historic cost is irrelevant. In making a decision whether to proceed with the project now, it does not matter whether the developer has made a capital gain or loss in the past (except that it may have tax implications for the developer).

The same concept applies whenever an investor is using an asset already owned as an input to a new project. For example, the asset might be existing plant and machinery being used for a new manufacturing project. The opportunity cost would be the higher of the asset's sale price or its value in an alternative use.

The converse applies if a valuable asset is to be retained at the end of a project when it might otherwise have been sold to create an incoming cash flow. This would include a property investment retained at the end of a development project. If an asset is retained, the value forgone is the potential net proceeds from its sale (or its value in an alternative use, if greater). This value should be attributed to the project as a notional incoming cash flow. In the appraisal of long-term property investments, it is often best to encapsulate value in a notional sale price (terminal value) within a sensible time-frame, rather than continuing cash flows indefinitely into the future.

The concept of opportunity cost is also important when estimating the cost of capital component of the required return. The general rule is that, where the actual direct cost of capital differs from the opportunity cost, it is the opportunity cost that is relevant. So, for example, if an investor was using capital raised on a long-term, fixed-interest basis some years before when interest rates were higher than at the present time, the historic cost is irrelevant. The opportunity cost would be the rate of return the capital would earn in an alternative profitable investment taking risk into account. That is the benefit forgone.

The opportunity cost of capital is particularly important when appraising investments to be undertaken by financial institutions, such as life assurance and pension funds. Money invested by these institutions does not have a direct cost, because it is not raised in the capital markets, but is received as regular payments from the contributors to life assurance and pension schemes. In Britain, it is conventional to assess the opportunity cost of investment capital by reference to the redemption yield available on long-dated government bonds (gilts). Gilt yields are a measure of the return available on virtually riskless alternative investments. This issue is examined again in Chapter 7.

THE PRINCIPLE OF INCREMENTALITY

It has been explained that costs or income that do not result from the decision to proceed with the investment should be excluded from the cash flow, and that opportunity costs should be included, even if they do not give rise to a cash flow. Finance costs should be incorporated into the required return, not the cash flow. Otherwise, the general rule is to include in the cash flow the value of all benefits and costs that are expected to arise as a result of the decision to invest.

However, not all benefits and costs will give rise to income or expenditure directly, or clearly attributable to the project in question. Where a decision to take on a project endows a benefit or imposes a cost on some other aspect of the investor's activities, the value of that cost or benefit must be attributed to the project by inclusion in the cash flow. The challenge is to identify the extent to which the project has an impact on other parts of the investor's business, and to capture the relevant costs and benefits in the cash flow. Defining the boundaries of a project's impact can be problematic in the case of companies with a range of integrated activities. But in the case of real estate, many projects are physically separate and, in most cases, 'ring fencing' the impact of decisions should be relatively simple.

None the less, any new project taken on is likely to impose 'overhead' costs, because, for example, of extra demands on management and office costs. Such costs attributed to a project's cash flow should be the additional, or *incremental* costs arising from the decision to invest. This is the general rule in estimating a project's cash flow. The economic cost of taking on a project is the extra cost arising from the decision. So, if existing management and head office facilities are under-employed, the incremental overhead costs of taking on a new project are likely to be low. But if an implication of taking on a new project is to employ new office staff, then these costs should be incorporated in the cash flow. It would be wrong merely to allocate some general proportion of overhead costs, or worse, to ignore these costs entirely.

PRACTICAL ECONOMICS VERSUS CONVENTIONAL ACCOUNTING

The rules about sunk costs and opportunity costs highlight the rational economic basis of DCF appraisal, and distinguish it from traditional decision-making techniques based on accounting profit and equity earnings. Discounted cash flow is practical economics, founded on economic logic. If an investment generates a return on capital greater than its cost of capital, economic value is created. NPV is a measure of an investment's expected economic value. If a project has an NPV of £1m, then a decision to take on the project will add £1m to the economic value of the company, which should be reflected in the value of its shares and, ultimately, in returns to shareholders.

Conversely, if an investment generates a return lower than its cost of capital, economic value has been destroyed, with consequential loss to shareholders. Hanson Trust, MEPC and Six Continents are three British companies that have been accused of the destruction of huge amounts of shareholder value by taking on investments that failed to provide a return in excess of the cost of capital. It was reported (Cohen, 1998) that in the five years to 1997, MEPC (which was formerly the second largest property company in the UK) destroyed some £1.2bn of shareholders' equity by earning returns below the cost of capital. Similarly, Six Continents plc (formerly Bass, the brewer) was accused by Hermes, the fund manager (Saigol, 2002) of destroying 'huge amounts' of shareholder value by over-paying for the acquisitions of the Intercontinental and Holiday Inn hotel groups.

Part of the reason for the failure of such companies appears to have been their reliance on criteria based on accounting profit when making investment decisions. That was the case with Hanson Trust, the Anglo-US conglomerate and apparently one of Britain's most successful companies until destruction of shareholder value led to the break-up of the company. Hanson was actively involved in taking over under-performing companies, adopting criteria based on accounting profit, focusing in particular on potential growth in equity earnings. An important criterion used to appraise investment projects was the Payback Period (Rudd, 1994).

Investment decisions based on accounting profit are unreliable, because profit is assessed, in part, according to non-economic rules and conventions – for example, by confusing historic cost with real economic cost, by manipulating the value of goodwill, and by ignoring the true cost of capital. In its heyday, Hanson could enhance its equity earnings by exchanging its highly-rated shares for the low-rated shares of the companies it acquired by take-over, but much of this earnings growth was accounting illusion, leading to the erosion of economic value and shareholder wealth.

Realisation that reliance on traditional accounting practice can result in uneconomic investment decisions has led to the adoption of new corporate performance criteria, such as economic value added (EVA), and to a new emphasis in business management on the maximisation of shareholder wealth. Growing acceptance of that aim reflects, not merely the power of capital, but a recognition that it is compatible with the promotion of business efficiency and an ability to compete successfully in a global economy. Maximisation of shareholder wealth implies that, if a company with surplus capital is unable to identify profitable investment opportunities, capital should be returned to shareholders. In fact, a company should use its capital to buy back its own shares if this offers a return above its cost of capital and more profitable alternatives are not available. It is a policy adopted by many large companies in the UK, USA and elsewhere.

SUMMARY

This chapter has introduced a number of further issues in project appraisal and has suggested a set of principles, rules and procedures for dealing with them. Specifically, it has:

- explained the need to undertake appraisal from the perspective and circumstances of the investor;
- outlined simple procedures for dealing with single-period capital rationing and project interdependence;
- emphasised the need to ensure compatibility between an appraisal's cash flow and required return;
- recommended a policy of excluding from an appraisal's cash flow any income or expenditure arising from a project's funding;
- identified the concepts of sunk costs and opportunity costs and, by reference to economic logic, explained why the former should be excluded from, and the latter included in, the cash flow to be discounted; and
- emphasised that a project's cash flow needs to incorporate all incremental costs and benefits arising from an investment decision, whether these relate directly to the project being appraised or impinge on some other part of the investor's business.

This has cleared the way to embark on the estimation of cash flows and the required return. These are the subjects of the next two chapters.

SELF-ASSESSMENT QUESTIONS

5.1 The six development projects illustrated in Table 5.3 have been appraised carefully and are expected to generate the cash flows and NPVs as shown. Assuming that:

- none of the projects is divisible;
- projects K and L are mutually exclusive, and
- capital expenditure has been restricted to £13m in Year 1 only

select the group of projects the developer should undertake.

Table 5.3 Development projects J–O

	Cash flows (£) *Year* 0	1	2	3	*NPV (£m)*	*Year 1 B/C ratio*	*Rank*
J	−5.0	−8.0	−10.0	+32.0	1.52	0.19	5
K	−1.0	−4.0	−3.0	+12.0	1.14	0.29	4
L	−2.0	−6.0	−2.0	+16.0	1.79	0.30	3
M	−4.0	−4.0	+10.0	–	0.08	0.02	6
N	−1.0	–	−4.0	+6.5	0.25	n.a.	1
O	−1.0	−1.0	−1.0	+10.0	1.68	1.68	2

5.2 Over the past few years a real estate developer has acquired a city centre site at a cost of £2.5m (excluding £0.5m spent on fees and site clearance), and is currently receiving a rent of £10,000 per annum after leasing the site for car parking on a short lease.

The developer has planned and carefully costed a development for the site that is expected to take 18 months, with the development being sold at the end of that period. The developer is confident that this proposal represents the site's optimal use.

Table 5.4 shows the expected net cash flow per quarter (three month period) representing the cost of construction and net income from the sale plus any rent received from tenants prior to the sale. The cash flow has been estimated after taking account of expectations for changing economic conditions including inflation.

In addition, the architect and surveyor are due to submit fees and expenses totalling £200,000 for the work involved in designing and costing the proposal so far. If the project proceeds, further charges of

Table 5.4 Net cash flow per quarter, construction and sale

Period	*Cash flow (£m)*
1	−0.5
2	−1.0
3	−1.5
4	−2.0
5	−2.0
6	+11.0

£500,000 for fees and expenses will be payable at the end of the project.

The developer's cost of capital is estimated at 10% per annum. It is judged that a premium of 8% per annum is appropriate to cover risk and provide the required level of profit.

As a result of falling market prices, the estimated value of the site is now £1.5m. If the developer decides not to proceed with the development and to sell the site, selling costs of 3% of the sale price will be incurred.

(a) Set out the cash flows from which you would calculate the project's NPV and expected IRR.
(b) Explain what discount rate should be used to calculate the project's NPV.
(c) Calculate the NPV and expected IRR for the project and advise the developer whether to proceed or not.
(d) Assume now that the developer feels more confident in estimating the required profit as a capital take-out on completion, and sets a target of £1.0m to cover the project's risk, illiquidity and a return for enterprise. What would be the revised cash flow and required return (per annum) for an appraisal on this basis?

Ignore taxation and any administration or other costs.

5.3 Prism Investments is a tax-exempt fund that owns Western House, a freehold office block let on a full repairing and insuring (FRI) lease expiring in seven years' time. The current rent is £150,000 per annum, paid annually in arrears. The current rental value is believed to be £165,000 per annum, and a rent review to rental value is due in two years. Prism believes that rental growth will average 4% per annum over the next seven years, and that the capital value should represent a year's purchase multiplier of ten. However, the building is becoming obsolete, and Prism is concerned about being able to re-let the property if the tenant quits at the end of the lease.

Prism has received an offer from the tenant to buy the property for £1.8m, which it believes to be somewhat above market value. Advise Prism whether to sell or retain Western House.

Assume that

- fees and expenses involved in the sale would amount to 1% of the sale price;
- no tax is payable; and
- Prism's required return on good quality office investments is 9% per annum.

ANSWERS TO SELF-ASSESSMENT QUESTIONS

5.1 The Year 1 benefit/cost ratios have been calculated and ranked, as shown in Table 5.3, helping us to identify the NPV-maximising group of projects. But they are not enough on their own; we must also use trial and error. Project N would be the first choice, because it has a positive NPV and no Year 1 cost. Project O would be selected next, because it provides an excellent benefit/cost ratio. Project L might be the next choice, but its selection excludes both K and J. (K because it is mutually exclusive with L, and J because this would take the Year 1 cost above the £13m limit).

By selecting K, despite its lower benefit/cost ratio compared to L, J can be undertaken within the £13m total Year 1 cost, resulting in a higher total NPV, as shown below:

Try: N + O + L + M NPV = 0.25 + 1.68 + 1.79 + 0.08 = £3.8m
Try: N + O + K + J NPV = 0.25 + 1.68 + 1.14 + 1.52 = £4.59m

The total NPV will be maximised by combining projects N, O, K and J. Therefore, these are the projects that should be selected.

5.2 (a) The economically relevant cash flow is shown in Table 5.5. The cash flow is explained below. The general rule is that the cash flow should reflect the amount and timing of all income and expenditure *arising as a result of a decision to proceed* with the project.

Table 5.5 Development project

Period (quarters)	*Cash flow (£m)*	*Discount factor*	*Discounted cash flow (£m)*
0	−1.455	1.000	−1.455
1	−0.500	0.960	−0.480
2	−1.000	0.921	−0.921
3	−1.500	0.883	−1.325
4	−2.000	0.848	−1.696
5	−2.000	0.813	−1.626
6	+10.500	0.780	+8.190
			NPV = +0.687

Period 0
The economic cost of the site is its opportunity cost; that is, the value forgone by using the site for the proposed development. As the proposed project is assumed to be the site's optimal use, the opportunity cost is the potential net proceeds from its sale – that is, £1.5m less 3% selling costs.

The historic cost of the site, its related costs and capital loss are economically irrelevant to the decision (except in so far as there may be taxation implications for the developer). Also, it would be wrong to take separate account of the £10,000 rent currently being received, because, while it is a benefit forgone from a decision to proceed with the project, its value will be reflected in the £1.5m potential sale price of the land. To include its value as well as the proceeds from the sale of the site would be double counting.

The architect's and surveyor's fees of £200,000 for work on the proposal so far are sunk costs and should be ignored. These are payable whether the project proceeds or not. These costs do not arise as a result of the decision to be made, and it is irrelevant whether these fees have yet to be paid or not. They are unavoidable whatever the decision.

Periods 1–5
These are unchanged from the figures given in the question.

Period 6
This figure is the cash flow given in the question (which is deemed to be net of the expenses of sale) less £500,000 to be paid to the architect and surveyor. These expenses must be

allowed for, as they result from the decision to take on the project. Note the distinction between the treatment of these fees and the fees incurred prior to a decision being made to proceed with the project.

(b) The 18% required return given in the question is per annum, whereas the cash flows are quarterly. These need to be reconciled in the discounting process. This can be done, either (i) by converting the 18% to an equivalent quarterly rate (see below) and calculating the discount factor in the usual way

$$\begin{aligned} r_q &= (1 + r_a)^{1/4} - 1 \\ &= (1.18)^{1/4} - 1 \\ &= 0.0422 \\ &= 4.22\% \text{ per quarter.} \end{aligned}$$

or alternatively, and more simply, (ii) the discount factors can be calculated using the annual rate, in which case n, the exponent in the discounting formula, represents years and part years. For example, the Period 5 discount factor is calculated as follows:

$$\frac{1}{(1 + 0.18)^{1.25}} = 0.813.$$

(c) The NPV is £687,000 as shown in Table 5.5. The IRR is 7.12% per quarter which, when annualised is:

$$\begin{aligned} r_a &= (1 + 0.0712)^4 - 1 \\ &= 31.67\% \text{ per annum} \end{aligned}$$

You might wish to check these figures. Some rounding error is inevitable.

As the project's NPV is positive and the expected IRR exceeds the required IRR, the project should be accepted.

(d) On this basis, the Period 6 cash flow would be reduced by £1.0m (=£9.5m) and the required return would be 10% per annum, the developer's cost of capital. As the cash flow is now net of the developer's required return for enterprise, risk and capital illiquidity, the required return must be made consistent with it.

5.3 The decision as to whether to sell Western House should be made by comparing the investor's required return with the expected return from retaining the property. In order to calculate the expected return, it is necessary to assume a notional sale at some future date. The question provides enough information to derive a terminal value at the end of the lease in seven years:

Expected terminal value, Year 7

Expected rental value, Year 7: 165,000 $(1 + 0.04)^7$ =	£217,129
Years purchase in perpetuity	10
Expected value, Year 7	£2,171,290

In order to complete the expected cash flow, it is necessary to calculate the expected rental income in Years 3–7 (after the rent review). This is the expected rental value at the end of Year 2:

165,000 $(1 + 0.04)^2$ = £178,464.

The relevant cash flow also needs to reflect the opportunity cost of retaining the property. This is £1.8m less the 1% selling cost, which is £1.782m.

This completes the investment's expected cash flow (see Table 5.6), which represents an *expected IRR of 11.6%* per annum. But what is the required IRR? This investment is obsolescent, and the lease has only seven years to run. It would not be classified as good investment quality, therefore a yield premium would need to be added to the 9% quoted. There is not enough information given to be precise about the required IRR, and as different elements of this investment are at different risk,

Table 5.6 Expected cash flow, Western House

Year	*Cash flow (£)*	*Discount factor*			*Discounted cash flow (£)*
		8%	*9%*	*12%*	
0	−1,782,000	–			−1,782,000
1	+150,000	0.926	–	–	+138,900
2	+150,000	0.857	–	–	+128,550
3	+178,464	–	0.722	–	+137,774
4	+178,464	–	0.708	–	+126,353
5	+178,464	–	0.650	–	+116,002
6	+178,464	–	0.596	–	+106,365
7	+178,464	–	0.547	–	+97,620
	+2,171,290	–	–	0.452	+981,423
					NPV = +50,987

there is a case here for calculating the NPV by using different rates to discount different elements of the investment (see Table 5.6).

The rental income in Years 1–2 is very secure and therefore has been discounted at a relatively low rate. The rent in Years 3–7 is less secure, because the expected rental growth of 4% may not be achieved – in fact, rents could fall. However, the terminal value in Year 7 is much riskier, because of the possibility of fluctuating rents and yields, as well as the risk of a prolonged void if the tenant quits at the lease end. Hence, the discount rate applied to that element of the investment has been raised to 12%. Even so, the NPV is positive, implying that Prism should retain the investment. However, the NPV is sensitive to the discount rate applied to the terminal value. If it is raised to 13%, the NPV is negative, implying a sell decision.

6

Estimating Cash Flows

OVERVIEW

It has been explained that DCF analysis essentially involves a comparison between the investor's expected return and required return. All we need to do in order to calculate a project's expected return is to identify the amount and timing of all income and expenditure, costs and benefits that are expected to arise as a result of the decision to invest. In other words, we need to estimate the relevant cash flows, and that is the subject of this chapter.

This chapter applies the techniques and principles introduced in earlier chapters to the practical context of property investment. It explains how such matters as growth, inflation, depreciation and taxation should be allowed for in cash flows, and illustrates the integration of theory and practice by means of an example of an appraisal of a substantial property investment.

DEALING WITH INFLATION AND GROWTH

In Chapter 5, we stressed the importance of compiling cash flows on the same basis as the required return. This is particularly important when dealing with inflation (or deflation). Conventional practice is to incorporate the expected impact of future inflation into cash-flow estimates, and to use a required return based on 'nominal' interest rates, also reflecting expectations about inflation. The alternative is to base the cash flow on current price levels; that is, to assume zero inflation and to adopt a required return based on 'real' interest rates appropriate to a world without inflation.

The NPV outcome and the investment decision should be the same in each case. If the latter method is used, the lower discount rate should compensate for the lower cash-flow estimates. However, the former method is much more popular in practice and is the one we shall use here. The better evidence available to estimate both cash flows and required returns normally gives greater confidence to decision-makers. For example, by including the impact of inflation in expected cash flows, we do not have to distinguish 'real' growth in rental income from growth generated by inflation. It is rarely practicable to make this distinction.

Generally, greater accuracy should be achieved by estimating cash flows as far into the future as is practicable. However, when estimating cash flows for long-term or perpetual investments, it is not practical to project them into the future indefinitely. Eventually, the cash flow should be brought to an end by a notional sale of the asset. This 'terminal' or 'exit' value should reflect the expected market value of the asset at that date, and thereby act as a proxy for the expected cash flow beyond that date. Only if an actual sale is anticipated should full account be taken of disposal costs such as expenses and capital gains tax. It is important to appreciate that a terminal value, if taken too early (particularly in the case of a low-yielding investment), can dominate the NPV and potentially invalidate the appraisal. It should properly reflect the likely impact of obsolescence at the notional date of sale and realistic growth prospects thereafter.

Investment decisions are for the future, and the future is uncertain. Implicit in every investment decision is a judgement about future risk and return, but in cash-flow appraisal, judgements have to be made explicit. The returns and risk from property investment and development are driven by the economy: local, national and international. Cash flows must therefore reflect expectations for the economy, and involve forecasting in some form. Forecasting techniques can range from sophisticated econometrics to intuitive 'guesstimates'; all are fallible but, like risk, forecasting is unavoidable. Whichever technique is used, it should involve a detailed investigation and analysis of the project's main variables and their determinants, taking into account all the likely consequences of a decision. But estimating cash flows is not an exact science. The outcome should be a *best estimate* (not a conservative one) and, inevitably, a judgement arising from the 'feel' that the appraiser gains from the investigation.

Substantial advances have been made in property market forecasting since the 1980s, and various organisations now provide forecasting services. However, it is an area beyond the scope of this book, and the reader is recommended to consult a text such as Leishman (2003).

There are dangers in making the cash-flow projection over-elaborate. For example, in many property investments, the most important variable is future rental growth, which can be disaggregated into growth related to inflation, real growth, and the impact of depreciation through obsolescence. This last variable might be subdivided, in turn, into physical, functional and economic obsolescence. If an attempt is made to quantify each of these variables independently, the outcome is unlikely to be more reliable than if the growth variable had not been disaggregated. The point is *not* that the appraiser should ignore the components, but that reliable quantification of each is unlikely to be practicable. As Hirst (2001) says, the 'objective is to be roughly right rather than precisely wrong'.

ALLOWING FOR DEPRECIATION

Like any other cost, depreciation of equipment, machinery and buildings through time, wear or tear, must be taken into account in cash-flow appraisal. In fact, dealing with depreciation of plant and machinery is simple in comparison with its treatment in conventional accounting.

To illustrate this, we shall assume that the net cash flow for Project A (originally introduced in Chapter 2) is broken down into the main components shown in Table 6.1. The table shows plant and machinery costing £50 at the start of the project in Period 0 and generating £10 from its sale (scrap value) at the end of the project (Year 4). The economic cost of the plant and machinery and its depreciation have been allowed for fully by these figures. If there had been no scrap value, the £50 cost in Period 0 alone would have allowed properly for the cost and depreciation.

By comparison, accounting practice, as well as the tax treatment of depreciation, is to write off a proportion of the historic cost of the machinery each year, perhaps 25%. Even if the machinery really did depreciate by 25% per annum, it would be quite wrong to include such an allowance each year in a cash-flow analysis. No actual cash flow takes place each year, and the machine's cost would therefore have been counted twice. Unfortunately, however, we cannot ignore depreciation allowances in DCF appraisal because they affect taxation, and tax is an actual cash flow. None the less, it is important to distinguish how a DCF appraisal allows for

Table 6.1 Project A: disaggregated cash flow

	Cash flow (£) *Years*				
	0	*1*	*2*	*3*	*4*
Plant and machinery	–50	–	–	–	+10
Other costs	–50	–10	–10	–10	–10
Income from sales	–	+30	+40	+60	+40
Net cash flow	–100	+20	+30	+50	+40

depreciation *per se* from how it allows for the taxation implications of depreciation. Both aspects are important.

In the case of buildings, the impact of depreciation is normally best dealt with in cash-flow appraisal by adopting rental growth rates and terminal yields that reflect expectations for depreciation, perhaps along with the estimated cost of refurbishment at some future date, if appropriate. The issue of depreciation and obsolescence in property is reconsidered in Chapter 8.

ALLOWING FOR TAXATION

In undertaking an appraisal with the objective of maximising the investor's wealth, it is important to reflect the investor's taxation liability. Preferably, we do this by allowing for tax explicitly in estimating both the cash flows and the required return; that is, by undertaking the appraisal on a net-of-tax (after-tax) basis. The alternative is to estimate cash flows and required returns on a gross-of-tax (before-tax) basis. In theory, the two methods should produce the same answer if, in the latter case, the higher discount rate properly compensates for the higher cash flow. However, in practice, a net-of-tax appraisal is likely to be more accurate. It is worth repeating the need for consistency between cash flow and the required return. If cash flows are net-of-tax, so must be the required return.

Taxation is a large and complex subject. It varies from country to country and between individuals, companies and institutions within a country. Important taxes affecting property investment in Britain include:

- Valued Added Tax (VAT);
- Stamp Duty, payable on the purchase of property at a top rate of 4% of the price (as of 2003).

One of the most important taxes affecting real estate in Britain is the tax paid on company profits, known as Corporation Tax. This tax encompasses taxable capital gain arising from the sale of assets as well as annual profits from business activities. Corporation tax is important to the real estate market, not only because it is payable by corporate property investors and developers, but also because property can provide a tax shelter to owners through capital allowances on plant, machinery and industrial buildings. By enabling investors to reduce their tax, these allowances, which have parallels in the USA and other countries, can have a significant impact on returns assessed after tax. Many property transactions are tax driven as a result of these allowances.

Corporation tax is a tax on profit. Profit is essentially income less allowable costs, including rent paid and interest on debt. For the examples in this chapter, we shall assume that the investor is a company, subject to a simple version of the UK tax paid at a rate of 30% in the same year as the profit is made. Note that, where the investor is a company, it is the tax payable by the company that is relevant in appraisal, not tax payable by the shareholder. The appraisal should be undertaken after corporate taxes, but before personal taxes.

Readers should note that the aim here is *not* to provide a guide to property taxation, but merely to illustrate how the impact of taxation may be incorporated into a DCF appraisal. In addition, at the time of writing, corporation tax is subject to review that may have a radical effect on capital allowances. In practice, the details are more complex than described here, and advice from an accountant or other specialist is recommended.

CAPITAL ALLOWANCES

The actual depreciation of property assets cannot be deducted from income for tax purposes in Britain. However, certain allowances are available instead. For the purpose of explaining these allowances, it is useful notionally to divide a property into the following three components:

(i) *Land*: land is deemed not to depreciate, so no allowances are available;
(ii) *Buildings*: buildings clearly do depreciate over time, but in Britain capital allowances are restricted to industrial, agricultural and certain other categories of building. In these cases, historic cost can be written off over 25 years on a 'straight line' basis; and
(iii) *Plant and machinery*: allowances are normally available on a 'reducing balance' basis.

Using examples, we shall now examine plant and machinery allowances and the Industrial Buildings Allowance (IBA).

Plant and Machinery Allowances

In Britain, an allowance is available on the notional amount by which the cost of plant and machinery is 'written down' annually. These allowances can vary, but we shall assume here a 40% first-year allowance on the cost of new plant and machinery, and 25% per annum writing-down allowances thereafter. In general, all qualifying expenditure of a company is included in a single 'pool', and the writing-down allowance calculated on the unrelieved expenditure at the end of the previous year, less any proceeds from sales of plant and machinery. If such proceeds exceed the written-down value of the pool, a 'balancing charge' is made. Conversely, where the plant and machinery is sold on cessation of the company's business, a 'balancing allowance' would be available if the proceeds of sale are less than the written-down value.

Example 6.1 illustrates the essential concepts, but see also Examples 6.3 and 9.1.

Example 6.1

A company is established to undertake a single project expected to last five years. Machinery costing £100,000 is to be installed in its property. Calculate the value of the annual tax allowances, assuming:

- a 40% first-year allowance;
- a 25% writing down allowance per annum thereafter;
- corporation tax is payable at 30%; and
- the machinery is sold for £10,000 at the end of five years, when the company ceases to trade.

The 'reducing balance' basis on which plant and machinery allowances are calculated is illustrated in Table 6.2. Allowances are deducted from income before taxable profit is determined; hence, at a 30% rate of corporation tax, their value is as shown in Table 6.2. Had the scrap value been nil in Year 5, the balancing allowance would have been £25,312. If the sale of the machinery had realised £30,000, a taxable balancing charge of £4,688 would have been made.

Table 6.2 Plant and machinery allowances

	£	*Value @ 30% tax*	
Cost of machinery	100,000		
40% first year allowance	40,000	12,000	Year 1
	60,000		
25% writing down allowance (WDA)	15,000	4,500	Year 2
	45,000		
25% WDA	11,250	3,375	Year 3
	33,750		
25% WDA	8,438	2,531	Year 4
Tax written-down value (TWDV)	25,312		
Sale of machinery	10,000		
Balancing allowance	15,312	4,594	Year 5

The following are examples of assets that may qualify for allowances in Britain:

- Equipment for ventilation, air conditioning, space heating and cold-rooms;
- Lifts, escalators and hoists;
- Surveillance systems, fire alarms and sprinkler systems;
- Moveable partitions and false ceilings;
- Furniture, toilet and kitchen equipment.

The significance of plant and machinery allowances to the property investor depends on the proportion of the property's price represented by plant and machinery. This varies substantially according to the property type. As a percentage of a property's cost *excluding land*, it can vary from virtually nothing in the case of a basic warehouse property, to over 50% in the case of refurbished air-conditioned offices, private hospitals or hotels. It is also significant in covered shopping centres, hi-tech industrial property and computer centres.

Industrial Buildings Allowance (IBA)

In Britain, capital allowances are also available to *owners* of buildings that are used for a qualifying purpose; essentially, manufacturing or a related activity. An annual allowance of 4% of the historic cost of the building is available over the first 25 years of the building's life. Unlike the reducing-balance basis of plant and machinery allowances, the straight-line basis of the IBA means that the annual allowance is a fixed amount over a fixed period. If a building cost £1m to build, the owner can claim £40,000 per annum for 25 years.

Industrial buildings allowances relate to the historic cost of the *building* only. If the original owner sells within 25 years of development for a price below the building's original cost, a balancing allowance or a balancing charge may be due. However, if the sale price attributable to the building is higher than the original cost, all allowances used must be repaid, and all allowances will accrue to the buyer.

Where a previous owner has repaid all allowances, or has not claimed the allowances, perhaps because this owner is a non-taxpayer, such as a pension fund, all allowances accrue to the new owner until the 25 years has expired. In this situation, an owner buying in Year 21 could claim 25% of the total historic cost of the building in each of the following four years. This could be a very valuable benefit and make a substantial impact on the price the buyer could afford to pay.

One might think that an owner would be unlikely to sell in Year 21 if faced with repaying the tax benefit received. However, the benefits to the buyer might generate a price that compensates the seller; alternatively, the buyer might be unaware of the tax implications of the sale. In fact, pension funds, since they are unable to benefit from the allowances, frequently make a point of selling before the 25 years have expired in order to gain the benefit of an inflated price.

Example 6.2

Twenty years ago, Alpha Engineering plc bought an industrial property on completion of its development for £1m, of which £800,000 was attributable to the building. Since then Alpha has claimed an IBA of £32,000 every year. It has just sold the property to Beta Manufacturing plc for £2m, of which £1.5m is attributable to the building. Advise Alpha Engineering and Beta Manufacturing about the taxation implications of the transaction to each firm.

Alpha engineering will now face a tax charge as follows:

$$\begin{aligned} &\text{£32,000} \times 20 \text{ years} &&= \text{£640,000} \\ &\text{Extra corporation tax to pay at 30\%} &&= \text{£192,000} \end{aligned}$$

The total IBA benefit now accrues to Beta Manufacturing, receivable over the remaining five years until Year 25:

$$\text{Annual IBA} = \frac{\text{£800,000}}{5} = \text{£160,000 per annum for five years}$$

At a 30% tax rate, this should reduce the company's tax by £48,000 per annum for five years.

The tax benefit of the deal to Beta Manufacturing may be reflected in the price paid to Alpha, failing which it might have been better for Alpha to have leased the property until the 25 years had elapsed, as no IBAs would be repayable thereafter. An IBA can only be claimed by the building's owner.

APPLICATION TO PRACTICE

In order to consolidate an understanding of the various issues raised in this chapter, Example 6.3 illustrates how cash flows may be estimated and compiled in the appraisal of a substantial property investment.

Example 6.3

Great City Estates plc (GCE), a major national property company, is appraising the Birches Mall with a view to acquisition.

The Birches Mall is a shopping centre well-located in a prosperous residential suburb of a British city. The property was originally developed in the 1980s, and was extended and comprehensively refurbished seven years ago. Its total lettable area approximates to 15,800m^2, and contains two foodstores (8,400m^2 and 2,800m^2), and forty retail units. It also comprises the manager's offices, twelve advertising stations and car parking (860 spaces).

The foodstores are both occupied by quality retailers. Other tenancies include many well-known national chains and reflect a good retail mix. Shop units are mainly let on 25-year or 15-year leases, subject to 5-year rent reviews to full rental value. However, the annual rent of Foodstore A is set at 1½% of turnover (total sales) in the previous year, subject to a minimum rent of 75% of rental value (25-year lease). Tenants are responsible for internal repairs to units, insurance of their fixtures and moveables, and local tax (rates). The advertising stations are let on a year-to-year basis.

Although two small shop units are currently vacant, they are expected to be let shortly. The centre has experienced increasing demand from retailers for tenancies in recent years, and is able to be selective in its choice of tenants.

The existing owner has made available certified accounts that provide details of income and costs over recent years. In addition, GCE commissioned a local-area analysis of the socio-economic structure of the population within the relevant catchment area. The analysis also investigated the potential for new housing development in the area, and the influence of competing shopping centres. This information has been combined with regional and national macro-economic forecasts to produce the rental and cost projections shown below under the heading of Further Information.

The Birches site is fully developed, leaving little scope for further exploitation. However, it is felt that, to maximise custom, development of the car park and improvements to heating, ventilation and security systems will be required over the next few years. Details are given under Further Information.

GCE is a major quoted real estate company which pays corporation tax at 30%, assumed to be paid in the same year as the liability arises.

Professional fees and expenses for the economic forecasts, local-area analysis and valuation are expected to amount to £80,000. If GCE proceeds with the purchase, stamp duty at 4% and legal fees at ½% of the purchase price would be payable.

The present owner of the Birches Mall has quoted an asking price of £50m. The objective here is to set out the net cash flow and calculate the expected IRR, assuming the property is purchased at that price. For simplicity, we shall assume a ten-year period of ownership, all cash flows occurring annually in arrears, and a notional sale in Year 10. At that date, it is assumed that the capital value will represent a yield of 8% on the property's rental value.

Further Information

Rental information is summarised in Table 6.3.

Recoverable Service Costs and Charges

Landlord's costs recoverable from tenants through service charges include: repairs, security, local taxes (rates), heating, lighting, insurance, cleaning and day-to-day management of the centre:

Total service costs (current year)	£850,000;
Service charges recovered (current year)	£830,000.

Service charges are allocated to tenants according to floor area occupied. This year's deficit largely reflects the costs attributable to the vacant units.

Non-recoverable Costs

These include the owner's costs of managing the investment (on site and head office), including professional fees for leasing and negotiating periodic

Table 6.3 The Birches Mall: current rentals

	Current rent (Year 0) (£)	*Estimated rental value (£)*
Foodstore A (turnover rent)	300,000	270,000
Foodstore B (rent review in Year 1)	670,000	900,000
Units C (rent review in Year 1)	300,000	400,000
Units D (rent review in Year 2)	520,000	680,000
Units E (rent review in Year 3)	600,000	770,000
Units F (rent review in Year 4)	400,000	450,000
Units G (rent review in Year 5)	140,000	150,000
Vacant units (H)		50,000
	2,930,000	3,670,000
Advertising stations	10,000	10,000
	2,940,000	3,680,000

rent reviews, rent collection, annual revaluation and performance measurement. Assume that these average 3½% of rental income per annum (before deducting rent voids and defaults).

Car Park

At peak times, the centre's car park is unable to cope with demand, and a third tier to the existing two-storey park is required. This has been costed at £1.3m (current prices). The work is expected to be undertaken in Year 2 and completed by the year-end.

Plant and Machinery

At the intended date of purchase, the tax written-down value (TWDV) of plant and machinery will be £480,000. In general, most of the equipment is adequate at present, but there is an intention to undertake substantial replacement of the centre's CCTV surveillance, ventilation and space heating systems in Year 3. This would be expected to cost £1.5m (current prices), and generate £20,000 from the sale of the equipment replaced.

No further replacement of plant and machinery is expected during the first ten years of ownership. Assume that a 40% first-year allowance and 25% writing-down allowances are available.

Forecasts of Rental Growth and Costs

- *Inflation*: GCE has been advised to assume an average rate of 3% per annum over the ten-year period to cover such matters as service costs and improvements;
- *Demand, turnover and rent forecasts*: The local economic analysis has produced optimistic retail demand forecasts for the centre. Retail turnover is predicted to grow at an average rate of 2½% per annum and rental values at 3½% per annum *on top of the rate of inflation* for both food retailers and others over the next ten years. However, an expected mild cyclical downturn over the next few years seems likely to have an impact on retailers occupying small units, resulting in some increase in rent defaults and voids from the current low level;
- *Service costs*: A detailed budget of service costs for the coming year, prepared at the request of tenants concerned about the charges, has revealed a 12½% increase next year. Thereafter, these costs are expected to grow at the general rate of inflation. The owner is responsible for the deficit unrecovered from tenants. This will tend to vary in line with rent voids and defaults.

Answer

The answer comprises the following components:

- Introduction;
- Spreadsheet (Table 6.4) showing cash flows for Years 1–10;
- Explanation of these cash flows;
- Calculation of P&M allowances, Cash Flow 17 (Table 6.5);
- Derivation of Year 0 cash flow;
- Derivation of Year 10 terminal value (Table 6.6); and
- Composite cash flow from which the IRR is calculated (Table 6.7).

Introduction

The objective is to set out the composite net cash flow and to calculate the expected IRR from this investment on the various assumptions given, including a £50m purchase price and a notional sale at the end of Year 10.

Table 6.4 details the various components of the expected annual cash flows in Years 1–10. Brief explanations of each are provided, together with a separate calculation of the taxation allowances for the plant and machinery. The total acquisition cost and expected terminal value in Year 10 provide the remaining figures to complete the cash flow from which the IRR is calculated. Note that no expenses of sale or tax on capital gain have been included in the terminal value, as the sale is notional.

Annual Cash Flows Explained

The notes below relate to Table 6.4.

Cash Flow 1
On the assumptions given, a rent for Foodstore A based on predicted sales turnover will exceed a rent based on 75% of rental value throughout the period. Hence, this cash flow is based on the current turnover rent, growing annually at the predicted sales growth rate of 5½% per annum.

Cash Flows 2–7
These cash flows are based on the current rents, rental values and rent review dates given (five-year review periods). Rental values are compounded at the predicted rental growth rate of 6½% per annum.

Cash Flow 8
The vacant units are assumed to be let shortly at their rental value on long leases subject to five-year rent reviews.

Table 6.4 The Birches Mall: cash flow, Years 1–10

Cash flow		*Year 1*	*Year 2*	*Year 3*	*Year 4*	*Year 5*	*Year 6*	*Year 7*	*Year 8*	*Year 9*	*Year 10*
Foodstore A	(1)	316,500	333,908	352,272	371,647	392,088	413,653	436,404	460,406	485,728	512,443
Foodstore B	(2)	900,000	900,000	900,000	900,000	900,000	1,233,078	1,233,078	1,233,078	1,233,078	1,233,078
Group C	(3)	400,000	400,000	400,000	400,000	400,000	548,035	548,035	548,035	548,035	548,035
Group D	(4)	520,000	724,200	724,200	724,200	724,200	724,200	992,217	992,217	992,217	992,217
Group E	(5)	600,000	600,000	873,353	873,353	873,353	873,353	873,353	1,196,570	1,196,570	1,196,570
Group F	(6)	400,000	400,000	400,000	543,577	543,577	543,577	543,577	543,577	744,748	744,748
Group G	(7)	140,000	140,000	140,000	140,000	192,970	192,970	192,970	192,970	192,970	264,386
Group H	(8)	50,000	50,000	50,000	50,000	50,000	68,504	68,504	68,504	68,504	68,504
Advertising stations	(9)	10,000	10,650	11,342	12,079	12,865	13,701	14,591	15,540	16,550	17,626
Total rent	(10)	3,336,500	3,558,758	3,851,167	4,014,856	4,089,053	4,611,071	4,902,729	5,250,897	5,478,400	5,577,607
Service costs	(11)	952,000	980,560	1,009,977	1,040,276	1,071,484	1,103,629	1,136,738	1,170,840	1,205,965	1,242,144
Service deficit	(12)	23,800	34,320	40,399	31,208	26,787	27,591	28,418	29,271	30,149	31,054
Rent voids, etc.	(13)	83,413	124,557	154,047	140,520	102,226	115,277	122,568	131,272	136,960	139,440
Management costs	(14)	116,778	124,557	134,791	140,520	143,117	161,387	171,596	183,781	191,744	195,216
Total deductions	(15)	223,991	283,434	329,237	312,248	272,130	304,255	322,582	344,324	358,853	365,710
Net income	(16)	3,112,509	3,275,324	3,521,930	3,702,608	3,816,923	4,306,816	4,580,147	4,906,573	5,119,547	5,211,897
Tax allowances	(17)	120,000	90,000	718,136	292,739	219,554	164,665	123,499	92,624	69,468	52,101
Corporation tax	(18)	897,753	955,597	841,138	1,022,961	1,079,211	1,242,645	1,336,994	1,444,185	1,515,024	1,547,939
Improvements	(19)		1,379,170	1,619,091							
Net cash flow	(20)	2,214,756	940,557	1,061,701	2,679,647	2,737,712	3,064,171	3,243,153	3,462,388	3,604,523	3,663,958

Cash Flow 9
Rents of advertising stations are reviewed annually and are assumed to grow at 6½% per annum.

Cash Flow 10
Cash Flow 10 = Cash Flows 1 + 2 + 3 + 4 + 5 + 6 + 7 + 8 + 9.

Cash Flows 11 and 12
Unrecovered service costs (12) have been estimated as a percentage of total service costs (11) which, in turn, have been estimated by reference to the current level, the predicted 12% increase next year and the predicted rate of inflation (3%) thereafter. The unrecoverable deficit will vary, largely in line with rent voids and defaults, which in turn will vary over the economic cycle. Under normal circumstances, the deficit is assumed to amount to 2½% of service costs, but in Years 2 and 4 an allowance of 3½% has been used, and in Year 3 it is 4%, reflecting the predicted cyclical downturn.

Cash Flow 13
Rent voids and defaults have been estimated as a percentage of total rental income (10). As in the case of Cash Flow 12, a normal rate of 2½% has been used, with 3½% in Years 2 and 4, and 4% in Year 3, related to the cyclical downturn.

Cash Flow 14
This is estimated at 3½% of rental income (10).

Cash Flow 15
Cash Flow 15 = Cash Flows 12 + 13 + 14.

Cash Flow 16
Cash Flow 16 = Cash Flows 10 – 15.

Cash Flow 17
See Table 6.5 for the calculation of taxation allowances. Note that this line is not an actual cash flow, but provides the basis for the calculation of Cash Flow 18.

Cash Flow 18
Corporation tax at 30% of the current year's net rental income (16) less allowances (17).

Cash Flow 19
Year 2 cash flow is the estimated current cost of the car park improvement compounded at the expected rate of inflation over two years. As an improvement, this is not tax deductable. Year 3 is the estimated cost of new plant and machinery compounded at the expected rate of inflation over three years, less the proceeds from the sale of the old plant and machinery.

Table 6.5 The Birches Mall: plant and machinery allowances

					Allowance	Year
Start Year 1	WDV		480,000	@ 25% =	120,000	1
			120,000			
Start Year 2	WDV		360,000	@ 25% =	90,000	2
			90,000			
Start Year 3	WDV		270,000			
Less sale proceeds			20,000			
			250,000	@ 25% =	62,500	
			62,500			
Old P&M	WDV		187,500			
New P&M	Cost	1,639,091		@ 40% =	655,636	
		655,636			718,136	3
			983,455			
Start Year 4	WDV		1,170,955	@ 25% =	292,739	4
			292,739			
Start Year 5	WDV		878,216	@ 25% =	219,554	5
			219,554			
Start Year 6	WDV		658,662	@ 25% =	164,665	6
			164,665			
Start Year 7	WDV		493,997	@ 25% =	123,499	7
			123,499			
Start Year 8	WDV		370,498	@ 25% =	92,624	8
			92,624			
Start Year 9	WDV		277,873	@ 25% =	69,468	9
			69,468			
Start Year 10	WDV		208,405	@ 25% =	52,101	10
			52,101			
Start Year 11	WDV		156,304			

Cash Flow 20
Cash Flow 20 = Cash Flows 16 – 18 – 19.

Cost of Purchase, Year 0

	£
Purchase price	50,000,000
Legal fees, stamp duty (4½%)	2,250,000
	52,250,000

Fees and expenses for forecasts, local area analysis and so on are all sunk costs. They do not arise as a result of the decision to invest, and are payable whatever the decision. Hence, they are economically irrelevant to the decision and should be excluded from a calculation of the expected return on which the decision is based. In contrast, the legal fees and stamp duty arise from the decision to buy, and need to be included.

This example has incorporated a number of assumptions that may be debatable. However, their validity is less important than the application of the techniques and principles explained in the text. Note that, in this case, rental growth has been forecast as a rate over and above inflation, contrary to the general recommendation expressed in the text.

A decision on whether GCE should buy the Birches Mall must await the estimation of the company's required return (see Chapter 7).

Table 6.6 The Birches Mall: expected terminal value, Year 10

Expected rental value, Year 10	£
Foodstore A	540,627
Foodstore B and Units C	2,440,278
Units D	1,276,453
Units E	1,445,396
Units F	844,712
Units G	281,571
Units H	93,857
Advertising stations	18,772
Expected rental value, Year 10	6,941,666
Capitalised in perpetuity at 8%	12.5
Expected capital value, Year 10	86,770,825

Table 6.7 The Birches Mall: calculation of expected return

Cash flow, years 0–10		£
Year 0 cost of purchase		–52,250,000
Year 1		+2,214,756
Year 2		+940,557
Year 3		+1,061,701
Year 4		+2,679,647
Year 5		+2,737,712
Year 6		+3,064,171
Year 7		+3,243,153
Year 8		+3,462,388
Year 9		+3,604,523
Year 10 net cash flow	3,663,958	
Notional sale price	86,770,825	
		+90,434,783

Expected IRR = 9.1% (by calculator)

SUMMARY

This chapter has started to bridge the gap between the theory and practice of cash-flow analysis. It has examined how issues such as rental growth, inflation, depreciation and taxation can be incorporated into cash flows, and illustrated these and various principles by means of a major example.

SELF-ASSESSMENT QUESTIONS

6.1 Summarise how the issue of depreciation should be allowed for in the DCF appraisal of property investments.

6.2 Assume that you are appraising a project expected to last five years, in which plant and machinery costing £1m is an essential part. Ignoring taxation, what cash flow would properly reflect the cost and depreciation of this plant and machinery in the following circumstances?

(a) The plant and machinery will have nil value at the end of the project, and will cost £10,000 to dismantle and remove.
(b) The plant and machinery will sell for £100,000 at the end of the project, but involve selling costs of £10,000.

(c) The plant and machinery will have a sale value of £100,000 at the end of the project, but will be retained for use in another project.

6.3 Distinguish the 'straight line' from the 'reducing balance' basis for determining annual allowances against corporation tax.

6.4 United Commercial Properties plc (UCP) is considering the purchase of Toll Junction Industrial Estate, well located on the periphery of a UK city, which is being offered for sale at an asking price of £1.0m.

Toll Junction is a small estate of five industrial properties, each of some 500 m^2 floorspace with appropriate office accommodation. The estate was developed almost 15 years ago by the seller, Nestegg Fund Management, which has not improved the property significantly since then. Costs attributable to the buildings totalled £600,000 (£120,000 each). Any original plant and machinery now has no value. As a tax-exempt investor, Nestegg has not claimed any Industrial Buildings Allowances (IBAs).

Unit 1 is occupied by a food processing business, Parsnips and Peas, which has installed and owns all necessary plant and machinery. The lease has twelve years to run at a current rent of £35 per m^2, subject to rent reviews in Years 3 and 8. The rental value is estimated at £45 per m^2. Food processing is not a qualifying use for IBAs.

Units 2 and 3 are both occupied by Polyplastic Extrusions. One unit is used for manufacturing and the other for the storage of raw materials and finished products. All uses qualify for IBAs. Polyplastic has occupied the properties since their development, and its current lease has 14 years to run at a rent of £40 per m^2, subject to review in Years 5 and 10. Rental value is £45 per m^2.

Unit 4 is currently unoccupied, but UCP is aware that Carrots and Cabbages is keen to lease a property of this size and location, provided that it is fitted out by the landlord with specialist plant and machinery at a cost of £30,000. On that basis, UCP would expect to be able to lease the property immediately for £50 per m^2 on a 15-year lease subject to five-year reviews. The property's previous use did not qualify for IBAs.

Unit 5 was about to be vacated by its tenant, Origami & Smith, at the end of its 15-year lease. The use qualified the property for IBAs, and partly because of the implications of this, UCP has agreed provisionally with the tenant to offer a 6-month rent-free period on a new ten-year lease (review in Year 6) at a rent of £50 per m^2, spend £10,000 on improvements and install plant and machinery at a further cost of £20,000.

In addition to the above expenditure, UCP anticipate an immediate need to install a CCTV security system costing £10,000 and to undertake improvements to the estate's roadways and parking facilities. This latter item would cost £40,000 at current prices, but will be delayed until the end of Year 2.

Current leases make the landlord responsible for external repairs and insurance, and this practice will continue with new leases. Together with ongoing repairs to roadways, and boundary walls and fences, such costs are expected to amount to £5,000 in the coming year. Management costs of £6,000 are expected to be attributable to the property in the coming year.

You are required to set out an estimated net-of-tax cash flow which would result from UCP buying Toll Junction at the asking price, and calculate the expected IRR.

The following assumptions should be made:

- All cash flows occur annually in arrears.
- Rental value growth is expected to average 2½% and inflation 3% per annum.
- Purchase costs resulting from a decision to buy would amount to 4½%, including stamp duty and legal fees.
- UCP pays corporation tax at 30% on net income, payable in the same year as the liability arises.
- First-year allowances of 40% and writing down allowances of 25% per annum are available on plant and machinery.
- Allow a notional sale of the property at the end of ten years.

Note: The years quoted for the timing of rent reviews (for example, Years 3 and 8 in the case of Unit 1) are the years (dated from the present) in which the increased rent will be payable, based on the rental value at the start of the year.

ANSWERS TO SELF-ASSESSMENT QUESTIONS

6.1 It is necessary to distinguish actual depreciation from depreciation allowances affecting the investor's tax liability. In considering actual depreciation, we simply need to address the cash flows to which depreciation gives rise. Depreciation of buildings, plant and machinery arises from obsolescence and physical deterioration. Hence, it gives rise to annual maintenance and repair, occasional renewal of components and, ultimately, substantial refurbishment or replacement. In so far as such expenditure can reasonably be predicted, it should be included in cash flows. However, a property's depreciation will also be reflected in its rental value (and hence its rental income) and capital value. Thus, the rental growth rate adopted for the analysis should reflect the impact of depreciation, as should the capitalisation yield used in estimating the terminal sale price (actual or notional) (see further discussion in Chapter 8).

Depreciation allowances are relevant to DCF appraisal because they affect the investor's taxation liability. Allowances for the notional depreciation of the building component of certain industrial, agricultural and other business properties are available in Britain to set against income, thereby reducing the tax liability. Allowances for the notional depreciation of plant and machinery in all types of business property are also available. In an appraisal undertaken on a net-of-tax basis, it is important to take into account the impact of such allowances on net-of-tax income.

6.2 (a) –£1m in Period 0 and –£10,000 in Year 5.
(b) –£1m in Period 0 and +£90,000 in Year 5.
(c) –£1m in Period 0 and, in Year 5, its value to the other project. Logically, this must exceed £100,000, otherwise it would be preferable to sell the plant and machinery.

6.3 The 'straight line' basis is used to assess allowances for depreciation of buildings structure, as in the case of the Industrial Buildings Allowance. The annual allowance is a fixed proportion of the building's historic cost. Hence, the annual allowance does not vary from year to year, and the tax written-down value will decline in a straight line if plotted over time.

The 'reducing balance' basis is used to determine annual allowances for depreciation of plant and machinery in Britain. After the first year, the allowance is a fixed proportion of the tax written-down value at the end of the previous year. Hence, for any item, the annual allowance will decline from year to year, and the tax written-down value will decline as a curve if plotted over time.

6.4 The answer comprises:

- Details of Year 0 costs;
- Details of the calculation of IBA and P&M allowances (see Table 6.8);
- Estimation of a notional sale price, Year 10;
- Spreadsheet showing components of annual cash flows, Years 1–10 (see Table 6.9); and
- Final net cash flow from which the IRR is calculated (see Table 6.10).

Purchase Cost and Year 0 Improvements

	£	£
Improvements, Year 0		
CCTV	10,000	
Unit 4	30,000	
Unit 5	30,000	
		70,000
Purchase price		1,000,000
Expenses of purchase, 4½%		
		45,000
Total cost, Year 0		1,115,000

Industrial Buildings Allowance

Total building costs = £120,000 per building
Units 2, 3 and 5 qualify, so, total IBA to claim over 10 years (to year 25)
= 3 × 120,000 = 360,000
= £36,000 per annum.

Estimated notional sale price, Year 10

	£
Year 10, net rental income	125,161
Years purchase in perpetuity at 12%	8.33
Estimated value, Year 10	1,042,591

The above calculation has adopted a high capitalisation yield to reflect the fact that the leases are running out in Year 10, and that the buildings will have suffered from obsolescence over the period. No selling costs have been allowed for, as there is no evidence to indicate that a sale will in fact take place in Year 10.

Cash Flows Explained

Cash Flows 1-4
These are calculated from the current rents and rental values given for Units 1–5, the projected rental growth rate of 2½% per annum and the rent review dates given.

Cash Flow 5
Cash Flow 5 = Cash Flows 1 + 2 + 3 + 4.

Table 6.8 Toll Junction: P&M allowances

	£		£	
CCTV	10,000			
Unit 4	30,000		**Allowance**	
Unit 5	20,000			
Total cost, Year 0	60,000	@ 40%	24,000	Year 1
	24,000			
	36,000	@ 25%	9,000	Year 2
	9,000			
	27,000	@ 25%	6,750	Year 3
	6,750			
	20,250	@ 25%	5,062	Year 4
	5,062			
	15,188	@25%	3,797	Year 5
	3,797			
	11,391	@ 25%	2,848	Year 6
	2,848			
	8,543	@ 25%	2,136	Year 7
	2,136			
	6,407	@ 25%	1,602	Year 8
	1,602			
	4,805	@ 25%	1,201	Year 9
	1,201			
	3,604	@ 25%	901	Year 10
	901			
TWDV	2,703			

Cash Flow 6
This is the estimated Year 1 cost of repairs and insurance given in the question compounded at the 3% projected rate of inflation.

Cash Flow 7
This is the estimated Year 1 cost of management compounded at the 3% projected rate of inflation.

Cash Flow 8
Cash Flow 8 = Cash Flows 5 – 6 – 7.

Cash Flow 9
Annual Industrial Buildings Allowance, (see p. 97).

Cash Flow 10
Annual Plant and Machinery allowance – see Table 6.8.

Table 6.9 Toll Junction Industrial Estate: cash flows, Years 1–10

		Year 1	*Year 2*	*Year 3*	*Year 4*	*Year 5*	*Year 6*	*Year 7*	*Year 8*	*Year 9*	*Year 10*
Rent Unit 1	(1)	17,500	17,500	23,639	23,639	23,639	23,639	23,639	26,745	26,745	26,745
Units 2/3	(2)	40,000	40,000	40,000	40,000	49,672	49,672	49,672	49,672	49,672	56,199
Unit 4	(3)	25,000	25,000	25,000	25,000	25,000	28,285	28,285	28,285	28,285	28,285
Unit 5	(4)	12,500	25,000	25,000	25,000	25,000	28,285	28,285	28,285	28,285	28,285
Total Rent	(5)	95,000	107,500	113,639	113,693	123,311	129,881	129,881	132,987	132,987	139,514
Insurance and repairs	(6)	5,000	5,150	5,305	5,464	5,628	5,796	5,970	6,149	6,334	6,524
Management	(7)	6,000	6,180	6,365	6,556	6,753	6,956	7,164	7,379	7,601	7,829
Net income	(8)	84,000	96,170	101,969	101,619	110,930	117,129	116,747	119,459	119,052	125,161
IBAs	(9)	36,000	36,000	36,000	36,000	36,000	36,000	36,000	36,000	36,000	36,000
P&MAs	(10)	24,000	9,000	6,750	5,062	3,797	2,848	2,136	1,602	1,201	901
Taxable income	(11)	24,000	51,170	59,219	60,557	71,133	78,281	78,611	81,857	81,851	88,260
Corporation tax	(12)	7,200	15,351	17,766	18,167	21,340	23,484	23,583	24,557	24,555	26,478
Improvements	(13)	–	42,436	–	–	–	–	–	–	–	–
Net cash flow	(14)	76,800	38,383	84,203	83,452	89,590	93,645	93,164	94,902	94,497	98,683

Cash Flow 11
Cash Flow 11 = Cash Flows 8 – 9 – 10.

Note: Cash Flows 9, 10 and 11 are not strictly cash flows, but provide the basis for calculating Cash Flow 12.

Cash Flow 12
Cash Flow 12 = 30% of Cash Flow 11.

Cash Flow 13
This is the estimated current cost of improvements to roadways and parking facilities (£40,000), compounded at the projected rate of inflation (3% per annum) over two years until the end of Year 2. It is not tax deductible.

Cash Flow 14
Cash Flow 14 = Cash Flows 8 – 12 – 13.

Table 6.10 Toll Junction: expected net cash flow

		£
Year 0		–1,115,000
Year 1		+76,800
Year 2		+38,383
Year 3		+84,203
Year 4		+83,452
Year 5		+89,590
Year 6		+93,645
Year 7		+93,164
Year 8		+94,902
Year 9		+94,497
Year 10 (net rental income)	98,683	
Year 10 (terminal value)	1,042,591	+1,141,274

Expected IRR = 6.92%

7

Estimating the Required Return

OVERVIEW

Cash-flow appraisal is a comparison between the return expected from an investment and the return required. Both are equally important. In Chapter 6, we examined the estimation of cash flows. In this chapter, we address the required return, with particular emphasis on the corporate investor.

As in the case of cash flows, the challenge is to *estimate* the required return, not to *calculate* it. There are too many imponderables to enable precise quantification; for example, the investor's cost of equity capital and the investment's risk. The formal analysis of risk and portfolio theory, other complex issues and fascinating controversies in finance are well covered by many excellent textbooks on financial theory, but this is not the place to examine them in depth. Yet, good practice in DCF appraisal cannot rely on a mechanistic application of techniques; it requires an understanding of the concepts and principles on which the techniques are based. Hence, this chapter invokes relevant principles from the theory of finance to underpin good practice. Initially, the chapter concentrates on a traditional view of the required return as a cost of capital adjusted to reflect a subjective assessment of risk. Thereafter, a more objective perspective is introduced, founded on modern portfolio theory, together with a variant of the NPV method of appraisal. Overall, the aim of the chapter is to assist the appraiser to make informed judgements, and to retain a healthy pragmatism about appraisal.

In practice and in textbooks, the required return is often called the 'target' return or 'hurdle' rate. Arguably, these latter two are preferable, as they acknowledge uncertainty of outcome, whereas the term 'required' return seems to imply certainty. In any case, all three are acceptable, and are now used interchangeably in the text.

COMPONENTS OF THE REQUIRED RETURN

An investor's required return is the expected return that is just sufficient to induce the investor to take on the investment. It is the minimum expected return acceptable to the investor. It will equate to returns available from alternative investments of similar risk, liquidity, duration and other qualities. Hence, it is an opportunity cost.

The required return may have three components:

- Investor's cost of capital;
- Extra return (yield premium or risk premium) to reflect the investment's risk, liquidity and other qualities; and
- In the case of projects (as distinct from existing investments such as bonds, equities and standing property), an extra return for enterprise.

It follows from the above that the required return depends on *both* the investor and the investment. First, we shall examine the case of institutional investors such as life assurance and pension funds, and, thereafter, the more complex issues surrounding corporate investors.

THE REQUIRED RETURN OF INVESTING INSTITUTIONS

The notion of the required return comprising three components is particularly useful in the case of institutional investors. We shall consider each component separately.

The function of institutions is to provide benefits to policyholders and pensioners, and the source of the capital used to acquire investments are the contributors to the policies and pension schemes. Therefore, unlike capital raised from banks or the financial markets, the investment capital used by institutions has no directly attributable cost. It is assessed by reference to its opportunity cost.

Redemption yields on conventional long-dated government bonds (gilts) provide a good indication of the opportunity cost of investment capital, particularly for property investment. This is because property and long-dated bonds are close substitute investments, of comparable duration and risk, and the certain redemption yields of fixed interest bonds means that these provide an identifiable measure of the opportunity cost of long-term investment capital. As gilts are traded securities, their redemption yields reflect the market's expectation for inflation. Thus, no further allowance for inflation should be made in estimating the target return.

It is conventional to assume that real estate investors in Britain require a yield premium of at least 2% over current redemption yields on long gilts to compensate for the perceived greater risk and poorer liquidity and marketability of property. The premium may also reflect the extra costs of transactions and management, and the different taxation treatment of property. However, if these extra costs are taken into account explicitly in cash flows, their reflection in a higher target return would result in double counting.

The yield premium required by property investors over gilt yields will vary according to the qualities of the individual investment being appraised. It will also tend to vary over time. In fact, evidence suggests that, in the 1980s, the yield premium might have moved over a range of some 5% in Britain (say, from a 2% premium to a 2% discount and back to a 3% premium), as perceptions changed about property's risk relative to bonds, caused by substantial fluctuations in inflation and other economic and market conditions (Fraser, 1986).

Evidence of the variation in yield premiums required by institutional investors from different UK properties is provided by a survey of institutional fund managers carried out by DTZ Debenham Thorpe (1997), see Table 7.1.

Reasons quoted for the different premiums included:

- lease lengths;
- strength of covenants;
- depreciation risks; and
- confidence about rental growth.

In other words, the prime issue distinguishing the required return between different properties is *risk*: risk of rent voids, tenant default, depreciation and lack of growth. Hence, higher premiums would be required in the case of poorer-quality investments, which are not attractive to institutional investors and were not included in the survey.

Table 7.1 Required premiums over gilt redemption yield

	%
Leisure property	4.0
Factories and warehouses	3.5
Provincial offices	3.5
Out-of-town shopping centres	3.25
Central London offices	2.75
High street shops	2.75

Source: DTZ Debenham Thorpe (1997)

There is an important difference between portfolio investment (for example, off-the-shelf investment in bonds, equities or standing property) and capital investment in projects (for example, property development). In the case of projects, the investor is acting as an entrepreneur and, in addition to the other components, will expect a return for his or her enterprise. In recent years, institutional investors have been involved increasingly in entrepreneurial activities through the provision of venture capital. Traditionally, a few of the largest funds have acted as property developers. It is impossible to be precise about the extra return required. It will vary from project to project, but a margin of between 5% and 10% would not seem to be exceptional. However, in the appraisal of property development, the return required for enterprise will frequently be represented by a capital sum (a negative cash flow at the end of the project) rather than as a premium on the risk-adjusted cost of capital.

THE REQUIRED RETURN OF CORPORATE INVESTORS

Estimating the required return of corporate investors (that is, companies, including property companies) raises a number of different issues from those relevant to institutions. First, capital employed by companies is raised through the financial markets, hence it has a directly attributable cost which must be covered by investment returns. Second, most companies employ debt as well as equity capital. These have different costs and tax liabilities, and the ability of companies to be geared (or leveraged) has further implications for their cost of capital and target returns.

Two alternative methods for estimating a company's required return are explained in this chapter. One is based on the capital asset pricing model (CAPM), but first, we examine the required return as a risk-adjusted weighted-average cost of capital (WACC). That is the average of the (after tax) costs of debt and equity capital, weighted according to the company's optimal gearing ratio, plus or minus a risk adjustment to reflect the investment's risk relative to that of the company.

We shall start by examining the costs of equity and debt, then proceed to explain the WACC via the concept of optimal gearing and the notion that the cost of capital relevant to appraising a project is not the cost of the capital employed in that project, but rather the cost of the company's 'pool' of capital. Finally, we consider the yield adjustment to reflect the project's risk.

THE DIRECT COST OF EQUITY CAPITAL

Equity capital is provided by shareholders, primarily through the purchase of new issues of shares, or by allowing the company to retain all or part of its annual profits (earnings). The return shareholders receive depends on the dividends paid by the company. The cost of equity capital to a company is essentially the same as the return paid to shareholders. More specifically, a company's cost of equity is the return that shareholders require.

The cost of equity can be viewed in two ways. First, by reference to shareholders' *expected* return, which is the sum of the prospective dividend yield and expected dividend growth, expressed as follows:

$$r_e = d + g_d \tag{7.1}$$

where $d = \dfrac{D_1}{P_0}$

Alternatively, the cost of equity can be viewed by reference to shareholders' *required* return, which is the sum of the returns available on riskless or relatively secure investments (such as government bonds), and a yield premium to compensate for extra risk. This can be expressed as follows:

$$r_e = r_f + r_p \tag{7.2}$$

In these expressions:

r_e = cost of/return on equity per annum;
r_f = risk-free return per annum;
r_p = risk premium per annum;
d = prospective dividend yield ;
g_d = expected dividend growth rate per annum;
D_1 = expected dividend, Year 1; and
P_0= current share price.

In an efficient market, such as the stock market, prices and yields will tend to adjust to give investors the (expected) return they require. So, the two methods of estimating the cost of equity should produce similar results. For example (see Example 7.1), if government bonds are yielding 6%, and shareholders in Alpha plc are thought to require a 4% risk premium, and if Alpha plc is expected to provide dividend growth averaging 7% per annum into the foreseeable future, *then* Alpha's (prospective) dividend yield must tend towards 3%, as follows:

Example 7.1

$$r_f + r_p = d + g_d$$

So,

$$\begin{aligned} d &= (r_f + r_p) - g_d \\ &= (6\% + 4\%) - 7\% \\ &= 3\% \end{aligned}$$

Alpha's cost of equity is 10% estimated by both methods.

The trouble with estimating the cost of equity by reference to expected returns is that the dividend growth rate expected (which, theoretically, should be constant in perpetuity) cannot be quantified accurately. Similarly, the risk premium is difficult to estimate, so the cost of equity cannot be calculated accurately by either method, but only estimated (however, see pages 114–17 for an application of the Capital Asset Pricing Model).

In addition to the 10% cost shown above, the cost of equity raised by a new issue is increased by necessary incentives and expenses. If a company raises equity by a rights issue to existing shareholders, a 'sweetener' will normally be required to persuade shareholders to buy the new shares. Normally, this would be provided by issuing the new shares at a price discount to the existing shares, thereby representing an initial yield premium. A new issue would also involve the payment of fees and expenses to professional advisers (such as lawyers, bankers and stockbrokers), plus an underwriting fee normally paid to an institution guaranteeing the successful sale of the new shares.

The total of such expenses would vary according to the size of the issue and the individual circumstances of the case. However, the total cost of Alpha's equity raised by a rights issue might be as shown in Table 7.2. The cost of equity capital raised by retaining earnings (profit) is essentially the

Table 7.2 Alpha plc: cost of equity by rights issue

	%
Prospective dividend yield, existing shares	3.0
Yield 'sweetener' on new shares, say	0.5
Expected dividend growth, per annum	7.0
Issue fees, expenses and underwriting, say	0.3
Cost of equity by rights issue	10.8

same as shown above, but excludes the yield sweetener and issue costs. Retaining profits rather than distributing them as dividends is a much larger source of equity capital than market issues but, because the capital is generated internally by the company, there is a tendency to feel that it is not new capital or that it is costless.

In fact, retained earnings could have been distributed to shareholders as dividends, and belong to shareholders in the same way as new money provided in a new issue. Hence, shareholders' required return on the capital (and thus its cost to the company) should be considered in the same way as for equity raised by a market issue, except that no expenses or sweetener are required.

Dividends are paid out of company profits after corporation tax has been paid; therefore, when undertaking an after-tax appraisal, no further tax adjustment is needed to calculate the cost of equity. However, it is important to appreciate that the simplified formula provided in Equation (7.1) assumes that dividends are paid annually in arrears; d represents the *prospective* dividend yield; that is, the expected dividend to be paid next year as a percentage of the current share price.

THE DIRECT COST OF DEBT CAPITAL

The cost of debt capital to a company tends to be substantially lower than the cost of equity, for two principal reasons:

(i) Lenders are willing to accept a lower return on capital provided. This is because their risk is lower, as debt is a prior charge over equity, both in payment of interest and repayment of capital;
(ii) Interest payments on debt can be set against profits in order to reduce the company's corporation tax liability.

Thus, in the simplifying case of irredeemable fixed interest bonds being issued by Alpha plc, the after-tax cost might be as shown in Table 7.3. The effect of the tax deductibility of interest on debt means that the cost of debt to the company is reduced by the amount of the tax rate. It follows from this that falling rates of corporation tax increase the cost of capital, and vice versa.

The relationship between investors' required yield on bonds and the net cost of debt tends to be more complicated in the case of redeemable (dated) bonds, because only interest payments are tax deductible, and not capital repayments. In the case of bonds priced at par (£100 per £100 nominal), all the investor's return comprises interest payments, therefore, as in the case of irredeemables, the company's cost of debt is the yield less the corporation

Table 7.3 Alpha plc: cost of debt capital

	%
Investors' required return on bonds, say	7.5
Add issue costs, say	0.1
	7.6
Less, corporation tax relief, at 30%	2.3
Cost of debt capital (after tax)	5.3

tax rate. However, in the case of dated bonds priced above or below par, a component of the redemption yield will be the (guaranteed) capital loss or gain to the redemption value of £100. The company's cost of debt capital is the IRR of the after-tax cash flow (interest and redemption value) paid by the company to the bond-holders until redemption.

The cost of bank debt is also tax deductible but, unlike debt raised by bonds, is usually provided on a variable interest basis. As interest rate changes are unpredictable, the future cost of such debt cannot be measured precisely.

THE CONCEPT OF OPTIMAL FINANCIAL GEARING

Debt has a variety of advantages over equity for a company wishing to raise capital. It is cheaper, and interest is paid from earnings before tax, while dividends are paid out of after-tax earnings. Debt is generally easier, simpler and quicker to arrange than equity, and, particularly in the case of bank borrowing, can be arranged in small amounts. By contrast, the costs involved in an equity issue mean that only substantial issues are economical. Hence, there is an incentive for companies to finance their expansion with debt rather than equity, and to become highly geared. However, debt capital has a prior claim over equity, therefore the higher a company's gearing, the greater is the risk to the company's equity, and the higher the cost of equity. In fact, beyond a certain level of gearing, any further borrowing could increase the risk to debt as well as to equity, and cause the cost of both to rise. Higher risk could cause the company's share price to fall, representing a cost to shareholders, even if no new equity was being raised.

Thus, further borrowing at high levels of gearing could impose indirect costs on shareholders, over and above the direct costs illustrated above. Conversely, raising more equity capital at high levels of gearing (by reducing gearing) could raise the share price, and effectively reduce the cost of equity below the direct cost illustrated above. These propositions represent the traditional view of financial structure, which asserts that there is an optimal level of financial gearing for any company, at which the company's cost of capital will be minimised and the company's value will be maximised.

The concept of optimal gearing is illustrated in Figure 7.1. The horizontal axis represents the company's gearing ratio, shown here as the value of debt as a proportion of the value of equity. The vertical axis measures the cost of capital. So, r_e and r_d represent the cost of equity and debt respectively at different levels of gearing, and $\bar{r}$ is the cost of the combination of debt and equity. At all levels of gearing, the cost of equity is shown to be well above that of debt, for the reasons explained above, but whereas the cost of debt only starts to rise at high levels of gearing, any increase above nil gearing is shown to cause a rise in the cost of equity.

The weighted average cost of the combination of debt and equity ($\bar{r}$) is shown to fall initially as gearing rises from nil. This is because increased gearing means the use of more cheap debt and less of the expensive equity. But after a certain gearing level, the combined cost of debt and equity starts to rise. The optimal level of gearing is represented by x, the trough of the $\bar{r}$ curve. At this point, the company's cost of capital is minimised and the company's value maximised.

This traditional view conflicts with the thesis of Modigliani and Miller (two famous names in the theory of finance), who concluded that in a no-tax

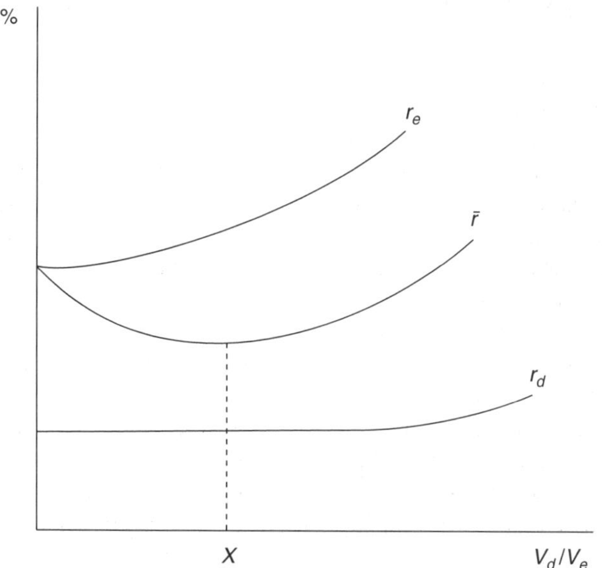

Figure 7.1 *Optimal gearing*

world, capital structure is irrelevant, but after taking corporation tax into account, companies should maximise their gearing, theoretically to 99.9%. In reality, company gearing averages around 25% (debt:total capital) and it is rare for debt to exceed 50%. Clearly, companies perceive some level of gearing as being beneficial, but high levels as being dangerous. This accords with the traditional view explained above, which is conventionally accepted, and is adopted here.

THE WEIGHTED AVERAGE COST OF CAPITAL

We are now making progress in our quest to identify the required return. A company's cost of capital is represented by the weighted average cost of the combination of debt and equity, at the company's optimal level of gearing. So, taking the costs of debt and equity for Alpha plc calculated above, and assuming that the company's optimal level of gearing is 30% (debt:total capital), its *weighted average cost of capital* (WACC) is:

$$(5.3\% \times 0.3) + (10.8\% \times 0.7) = 9.15\%$$

In calculating the WACC, we applied the following formula, which emphasises that the weightings of debt and equity should normally be based on the *market value* of debt and equity rather than on nominal amounts:

$$r_{\text{wacc}} = r_d\,(1 - T)\,\frac{V_d}{V_e + V_d} + r_e\,\frac{V_e}{V_e + V_d} \qquad (7.3)$$

where:

r_d = cost of debt (before tax adjustment);
r_e = cost of equity;
V_d = market value of debt capital;
V_e = market value of equity capital; and
T = rate of corporation tax.

One problem in estimating a company's WACC is that it is not practicable to identify accurately the optimal level of gearing at any point in time. It will vary according to the company's activities; for example, food retailers face a relatively stable demand and can afford high gearing, but for companies such as property developers, operating in a cyclical market, high gearing is risky. The optimal level of financial gearing also depends on the company's operational gearing. This reflects other fixed costs that are prior liabilities for a company – for example, rental payments. Corporate risk is more a function of the combination of operational gearing and financial gearing than financial gearing *per se*.

Optimal gearing will also vary over time. In times of economic recovery and expansion, when demand is rising and interest rates are low, high gearing will boost earnings. But when a recession is threatened and interest rates are rising, high gearing is particularly risky.

In an ideal world, a company would identify its optimal gearing and stick to it, funding new investments with debt and equity in the optimal proportion. But in reality, the optimal ratio is not clearly identifiable, nor is it practicable or economical to raise equity or long-term debt in small amounts. Therefore, a company will tend to set a target level of gearing that it regards as optimal, and finance new investments either with equity or debt, bearing the target ratio in mind. This will result in the actual gearing fluctuating above and below the target level. For example, if a company's gearing is above target, and substantial new capital is required for a new project, it would tend to raise new equity, but if gearing is below target, the project would tend to be funded with debt.

Assume now that Alpha plc has to accept or reject an investment with an expected IRR of 8%. Should Alpha accept the proposal if it is to be funded with debt (cost 5.3%) and reject it if funded by equity (cost 10.8%)? Following that rationale, if Alpha accepts this project with debt funding, the next project might have to be funded by equity (to maintain the target gearing), and would have to be rejected even if it offered an expected IRR of 9%, higher than the first project. Clearly, therefore, investment decisions should *not* be based on the direct cost of the capital used to fund the investment, because these direct costs do not reflect the true opportunity cost of the capital. Indirect costs and benefits mean that the true cost of debt is greater than the direct cost, and the true cost of equity is below its direct cost. The true cost of capital is represented by the company's WACC at the target gearing ratio. Even if a project is funded by debt or equity alone, the project's target return should be based on the company's WACC. Notionally, investments should be considered as being funded out of the company's 'pool' of capital, debt and equity, and a project should be appraised in isolation from its actual funding. Referring back to Chapter 5 (see page 65), this provides another reason for rejecting the practice of including debt interest and capital repayment in a project's cash flow.

ADJUSTING THE WACC FOR RISK

The return that a company needs to earn from its business activities is the return necessary to pay shareholders (and bond-holders) the return they require, taking risk into account. By deriving the WACC from the returns required by investors in the company's equities and bonds (see page 104 – 'The Direct Cost of Equity Capital', and page 107 – 'The Direct Cost of Debt Capital'), allowance has been made for the company's risk, as perceived by stock market investors. In fact, assuming that the company's activities are entrepreneurial (for example, a property developer), the WACC incorporates all three elements of the required return outlined on page 102 – 'Components of the Required Return'. Therefore, in the case of a project that is typical of the company's activities, and of a similar risk to the company as a whole (which will reflect its gearing as well as its projects), the unadjusted WACC will represent the appropriate required return. However, if the investment being appraised is deemed to have a greater risk than the risk of the company as a whole, a risk premium should be added to the WACC; or, if the investment is considered to be less risky, a deduction should be made.

Assessment of the appropriate risk premium or discount in any particular case is necessarily subjective. An important issue is that the risk adjustment should reflect the investment's relative risk in the context of the company's overall portfolio of projects or activities, and not the risk of the new investment in isolation. If the new investment is independent of existing activities, its returns may not be correlated with those of the company, and may thereby reduce the company's risk even if the investment is risky in isolation. This issue increases the difficulty of making an appropriate risk adjustment.

APPLICATION OF THE RISK-ADJUSTED WACC

Example 7.2 is provided to illustrate the estimation of a required return by means of a risk-adjusted WACC. The context is the same as that used in Example 6.3 in Chapter 6 (see page 84).

Example 7.2

Refer back to Example 6.3 and assume the following further information about Great City Estates plc (GCE).

GCE is a major listed real estate company with a substantial property portfolio composed mainly of industrial and office properties. It also undertakes property development, but 85% of its capital is invested in standing properties.

It maintains a target gearing ratio of 20% (debt:total capital) which is believed to be optimal. Most debt has been raised by long-dated bonds. Those priced at par currently yield 6.3%.

The company's shares are currently priced at £1.10, a year-end dividend of three pence per share has recently been paid, and the company's stockbrokers are forecasting dividend growth averaging 7% per annum into the foreseeable future.

The purchase of the Birches Mall would be financed from capital reserves. GCE pays corporation tax at 30%, assumed to be paid in the same year as the liability arises.

- Estimate the target return that would be appropriate to the appraisal of the Birches Mall, by estimating GCE's risk-adjusted WACC.
- Based on the expected IRR calculated in Example 6.3, advise GCE whether to buy the Birches Mall at the asking price of £50m.

Answer

Cost of equity

Information is given to enable the cost of equity to be estimated by reference to the prospective dividend yield and forecast dividend growth:

$$r_e = \frac{D_1}{P_0} + g_d$$

$$D_1 = 3p\,(1 + 0.07) = 3.21p$$

$$r_e = \left(\frac{3.21}{110} \times 100\right) + 7.0\% = 9.92\%$$

Cost of debt

$$6.3\%\,(1 - 0.3) = 4.41\%$$

WACC

This is the average of the costs of equity and debt, weighted according to the target gearing ratio:

$$(0.8 \times 9.92\%) + (0.2 \times 4.41\%) = 8.8\%$$

Note: The investment is to be financed out of existing capital resources, so no issue expenses should be included in the cost of capital.

Risk adjustment

In order to estimate the target return, the WACC needs to be adjusted up or down to reflect the risk of this investment relative to that of GCE.

The Birches Mall appears to be a sound standing investment which, as a retail property, may prove to have a low correlation with GCE's existing portfolio. In addition, a significant part of the company's activities involve risky development. Hence, the Birches Mall appears relatively secure, and a small yield discount on the WACC seems appropriate:

$$\text{Target return} = 8.8\% \text{ less, say } 0.5\% = 8.3\%.$$

As the target IRR is below the expected IRR (9.1%), a buy decision is indicated.

THE CAPM AND THE COST OF EQUITY CAPITAL

The purely subjective basis of the risk adjustment to the WACC and the need to consider risk in the portfolio context provide important arguments for assessing an investment's target return using the capital asset pricing model (CAPM). The CAPM also provides a more objective basis for estimating the cost of a company's equity capital. On page 105, it was explained that a company's cost of equity could be estimated either:

- by reference to shareholders' expected return, which requires an estimation of future dividend growth; or
- by reference to shareholders' required return, which involves an estimation of the required risk premium.

Whereas a reasonable estimate of future dividend growth can sometimes be gleaned from company forecasts or from historic growth performance, no objective means of estimating the risk premium has so far been put forward. That objectivity, together with a certain academic authority, is provided by the CAPM. The general concept of the CAPM is now outlined, but readers who are unfamiliar with the model are recommended to refer to one of the many textbooks in financial theory that examine the subject in greater depth.

Investors are concerned primarily with risk and return, and require higher returns from investments with higher risk. By determining market prices from the buy and sell decisions of investors, the stock market prices the relationship between risk and return; or, more specifically, the stock market prices the trade-off between investors' *perceived* risk and their *expected* return. It is the relationship between risk and return that is defined by the CAPM.

Most stock market investors do not hold shares singly; they hold portfolios or collections of shares, because diversification reduces risk. But diversification cannot eliminate risk, hence the distinction in modern portfolio theory (MPT) between;

- *specific risk*, which can be avoided by diversification; and
- *market (or systematic) risk*, which cannot be avoided as it derives from fluctuations in share prices in general – that is, upward and downward movements of the stock market.

Because of the ease with which specific risk can be avoided (20–30 shares equally weighted should avoid 90% of such risk), it should be disregarded by investors in their buy/sell decisions, and therefore should not be reflected in market prices. Only market risk should be impounded in share prices. A share's market risk derives from fluctuations in the equity market, but shares are not affected equally – some are more sensitive than others to fluctuations. This sensitivity – that is, a share's market risk relative to the equity market as a whole – is measured by the beta (ß) coefficient. A share with a beta of 0.5 would be half as volatile as the equity market, and a share with a beta of 1.5 would be 50% more volatile than the market.

The CAPM defines the relationship between an investment's expected return and its beta by reference to the risk-free return and the market's expected risk premium (that is, the extra return that shares in general are expected to earn over and above returns from riskless investments). The CAPM establishes a simple linear relationship between expected return and market risk, as defined below and illustrated in Figure 7.2.

$$Er_s = r_f + \beta_s (Er_m - r_f) \tag{7.4}$$

where: Er_s = expected return from share s;
r_f = return available on riskless investments;
β_s = beta of share s; and
Er_m = expected return from the share market.

The CAPM enables us to calculate the cost of a company's equity because the cost of equity is shareholders' required return, which is an opportunity cost – that is, the return expected from an investment of similar risk. As indicated on page 104 – 'The Direct Cost of Equity Capital', the required return comprises a risk-free return and a risk premium. In the CAPM, the risk premium is defined as the product of the investment's beta and the

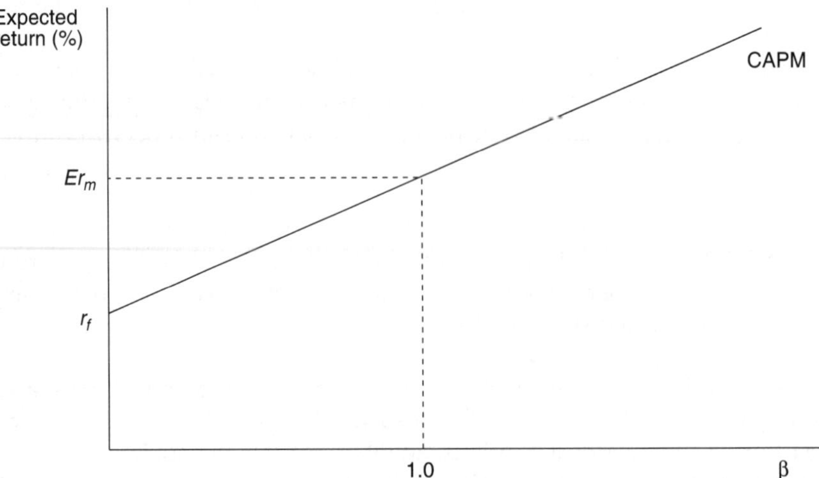

Figure 7.2 *Capital asset pricing model*

market's expected risk premium ($Er_m - r_f$). The CAPM is an *ex-ante* model; that is, it is a statement about expected return in the future.

The betas of shares listed on the London Stock Exchange are measured on a regular basis and published, for example, by the London Business School. The risk-free return can be taken as the current return on Treasury bills or government bonds (gilts). However, because of the difficulty of estimating the market's expected risk premium (looking forward), this is often taken as the long-term historic excess return provided by the equity share market. According to Barclays Capital (2000), the extra return earned by equity shares over the return from gilts averaged 4.7% per annum in the twentieth century. The excess return over Treasury bills averaged 4.1% per annum. Using this information, we can calculate the cost of equity for any company for which a beta is available.

Example 7.3

Calculate the cost of equity for Alpha plc, assuming its beta is 1.06, the current yield on gilts is 5%, and the equity risk premium is 4.7% per annum:

$$Er_s = r_f + ß_s (Er_m - r_f)$$
$$Er_s = 5\% + (1.06 \times 4.7\%)$$
$$= 10.0\%$$

As with previous methods for estimating the cost of equity, no adjustment should be made to this calculation to reflect corporation tax in an after-tax appraisal, because shareholders' returns are after-tax *per se*.

The principal merit of the CAPM is to define in a simple equation the relationship between risk and return for marketable investments. However, it may be more valuable as a concept than as a means of calculating the cost of equity or of a project's required return (see below). Various criticisms could be made of the above application of the model; for example, the equity market's risk premium (ERP) looking forward is not likely to be the historic ERP averaged over a hundred years. It will vary over time, and the periods of high inflation that have been partly responsible for the historic ERP are not likely to be repeated in the foreseeable future. Other reasons to be cautious are that a company's beta need not remain stable over time, and that the CAPM is based on a number of assumptions of dubious validity (see page 124). On the other hand, the model is now widely used by investment analysts. At worst, the beta provides an objective market measure of the *relative* risk of companies, and the model brings a different perspective for estimating the cost of equity to supplement that outlined on pages 104–7.

USING THE CAPM TO ESTIMATE A PROJECT'S REQUIRED RETURN

The CAPM defines the relationship between risk and return, and is potentially applicable to any investment for which a beta can be estimated. If we can estimate the beta of an individual property investment or development project, we could use the CAPM to reflect risk in the investment's required return. Risk would be incorporated into the appraisal objectively, compared to the intuitive subjectivity on which the WACC method relies.

Equity share betas can be measured easily from their price movements relative to the market. But that is not possible in the case of individual property investments or projects, because they are not traded regularly. None the less, it is possible to estimate the betas of typical investments from company share betas. The process is based on the notion that a company is essentially a portfolio of business assets incorporated. In addition, most companies are geared. Therefore, the risk of a company's equity arises from two sources:

- Risk arising from the business assets (including operational gearing); and
- Risk arising from financial gearing.

By stripping out the effect of financial gearing from the company beta (degearing), the beta of the underlying business assets can be identified. If these assets are relatively homogeneous, then the beta of the typical asset can be identified, and the CAPM can then be used to estimate the required return appropriate to the appraisal of such an asset.

The beta of a company's assets is the weighted average of the betas of the securities that finance the assets:

$$ß_{assets} = ß_e \frac{V_e}{V_e + V_d} + ß_d \frac{V_d}{V_e + V_d} \qquad (7.5)$$

where V_e = market value of equity capital;
V_d = market value of debt capital;
$ß_e$ = beta of the company's equity shares; and
$ß_d$ = beta of the company's debt.

Two adjustments are usually made to the above equation. First, because of the priority of debt over equity, equity bears most of the risk and, in normal circumstances, it is conventional to assume that the debt capital is virtually riskless. Hence, the second part of the equation is omitted. Second, as the tax deductibility of interest payments effectively reduces the impact of gearing on the risk of equity, the weighting of debt capital is reduced by the amount of the tax relief. Therefore, the relationship between the beta of a company's assets and its equity shares is amended as follows:

$$ß_{assets} = ß_e \frac{V_e}{V_e + V_d (1 - T)} \qquad (7.6)$$

where T = corporation tax rate

By solving this equation, the betas of typical investments or projects can be estimated from the share betas of companies engaged in these activities. For example, the beta of housing development would be derived from the betas of house builders; the beta for office investments would be derived from companies whose principal activity was office investment, and the beta for commercial property development would be derived from the betas of property development companies.

Example 7.4

Calculate the target return appropriate for the appraisal of a standing office investment which is considered to be typical of investments held by two property companies, A and B, whose equity betas, gearing and market capitalisation are given in Table 7.4. Assume a corporation tax rate of 30%, a risk-free rate of 4% and an equity risk premium of 6%.

Table 7.4 Companies A and B

	Equity Beta	*Gearing (by value)*		*Market capitalisation (£m)*
		Debt (%)	*Equity (%)*	
Company A	1.08	25	75	700
Company B	1.30	40	60	300

Answer

First, using Equation (7.6), calculate the assets' beta for each company and then find the weighted average asset beta, reflecting the relative sizes of the two companies.

$$\text{Company A:} \quad ß_{\text{assets}}\ 1.08 \left[\frac{75}{75 + 25(1 - 0.3)} \right] = 0.876$$

$$\text{Company B:} \quad ß_{\text{assets}}\ 1.30 \left[\frac{60}{60 + 40(1 - 0.3)} \right] = 0.886$$

Weighted average asset beta = (0.876 × 0.7) + (0.886 × 0.3) = 0.88.
Now calculate the after-tax required return using the CAPM:

$$\begin{aligned} E_r &= r_f + ß\,(Er_m - r_f) \\ &= 4\% + (0.88 \times 6\%) \\ &= 9.3\% \end{aligned}$$

That would be the target return on an assumption of equity-only financing. If, however, the appraisal assumed a combination of debt and equity, the cost of equity element would be raised by the gearing, and would be found by *re-gearing* – that is, reversing the de-gearing process – at the relevant capital mix.

A major simplification in the example above is that the investment to be appraised is assumed to be typical of the investments held by the companies from which the beta was derived. That would be unusual and fortunate. Most real estate companies undertake a diversity of activities, including development (high risk) and investment (low risk), and it is not always easy to identify a typical investment. Adjustments will therefore have to be made in selecting the beta for an investment which is felt to have a different market risk from the activities typical of the companies from which the beta is derived.

In making such an adjustment, it is important to bear in mind the factors that give rise to market risk. An investment's market risk reflects the sensitivity of its return to returns from the equity market generally. Market returns reflect, for example, trends in interest rates and corporate profitability. Hence, an investment's beta will reflect the sensitivity of the investment's net cash flows to general trends in interest rates, corporate profits and the economy in general.

The main variables determining the return from a standing property investment are rental income, rental value and market yield. These are all sensitive to macro-economic conditions. However, the sensitivity will be substantially less in the case of a prime property let on a long lease on upward-only rent reviews to a reliable tenant than in the case of a secondary property where the lease is nearing its end.

An important factor determining beta is the investment's operational gearing; that is, the extent to which fluctuations in net cash flows are exacerbated by fixed costs or prior charges. Returns from property development are a highly geared and volatile residual. Development profit is essentially the property's value on completion, less construction, finance and other development costs. The market risk of a development is the market risk of the completed property, exacerbated by the fact that a high percentage of the value on completion is a prior charge. The market risk of development is increased by the fact that all main variables (rental value, yield, construction and finance costs, duration until let) are cyclical. These tend to move simultaneously, either beneficially or adversely over the cycle. During an economic upturn, when business is doing well, property values tend to rise and development costs may be stable. However, during an economic downturn, property values tend to fall and costs may be rising.

The sensitivity of development profit to macro-economic change, in part because of the inherent operational gearing, creates high market risk, implying high target returns. But operational gearing can also play a part in standing investments, particularly where the investor retains a responsibility for repairs, insurance and management of properties that have multiple-occupancy. These costs would be an unavoidable charge on rental income, which could result in net income being more sensitive to rental trends than gross rental income.

THE ADJUSTED PRESENT VALUE METHOD

Apart from the subjective assessment of risk, estimating a target return as a risk-adjusted WACC involves a number of simplifying assumptions or approximations. Underlying assumptions are that projects and debt are perpetual (the latter with constant tax benefits), and that the optimal level of gearing remains unchanged after the new project is taken on. But, in reality, a decision to take on a new investment will affect a company's ability to borrow, and may change its optimal gearing ratio. For example, a decision to take on a large secure property investment may result in a significant increase in the investor's borrowing capacity. Because of the relative cheapness of debt, that has value which needs to be reflected in the appraisal. That value is quantified separately and explicitly in the adjusted present value (APV) method.

In most cases, the inaccuracies resulting from the estimations and assumptions implicit in the WACC will be less significant than the inevitable inaccuracies resulting from other sources. None the less, the APV method has the advantage of revealing the individual costs and benefits arising from a decision to take on an investment. It also exploits the objectivity of the CAPM in allowing for risk.

The APV is a variant of the NPV method, but instead of adjusting the target return to reflect financing implications, it is the NPV that is adjusted. This may be more accurate, particularly in complex cases. The APV method is based on the principle of 'value additivity'; that is, the value of the whole is the sum of the value of the parts. In the case of an individual investment, the APV is the sum of the NPVs (positive and negative) that arise from the various aspects of the investment and its financing. The process is to value the investment as if it were financed solely by equity, then to add (or subtract) the NPV value (or cost) of the financing implications of the investment.

We shall illustrate the process by developing the situation previously used in Example 7.4.

Example 7.5

Assume that the office investment in Example 7.4 is for sale valued at £20m, and has recently been let to a single tenant at a net rent of £1m per annum, payable annually in arrears, and that its rental and capital value is expected to grow at an average of 6% per annum. Company C proposes to acquire the property for £20m, but intends to finance it by means of a new equity issue, the expenses of which will amount to 2½% of the capital raised (assumed to be tax allowable). The acquisition is estimated to have a borrowing capacity of £14m. The company can borrow at 7% fixed interest.

Company C pays tax at 30% (paid in the same year as the income is received). Assume, for simplicity, that the property will be sold at the first rent review in five years' time, no tax will be payable on the capital gain realised, no taxation allowances are available, and that the buying and selling costs of the property can be ignored.

Answer

The first stage is to establish the 'base-case' NPV of the investment – that is, the NPV as if it were fully financed by existing equity. In Example 7.4, we identified the required return on this basis as 9.3%, so, in order to calculate the NPV, we must estimate the net cash flow and discount it at 9.3%, as shown in Table 7.5.

In order to arrive at the APV, we have now to add or subtract the value or cost of the financing side-effects of the investment. There are just two matters to be taken into account here: the expenses of the equity issue and the value of the potential tax shield that arises as a result of the debt capacity introduced by taking on the investment. Despite the fact that this borrowing capacity is not being used to finance the purchase directly, it has value in raising the company's borrowing capacity for a future investment. This needs to be taken into account in the decision process.

Issue expenses

One must assume that an equity issue is a prudent consequence of the investment, hence allowance needs to be made for the issue costs. In order to raise £20m net of expenses at 2½%, £20.513m needs to be raised. The expenses of £513,000 are equivalent to £359,000 after tax. We shall

Table 7.5 Example 7.5: Office investment

	Expected cash flows (£m) *Year*					
	0	*1*	*2*	*3*	*4*	*5*
Purchase and sale	–20.000	–	–	–	–	+26.765
Rental income	–	+1.000	+1.000	+1.000	+1.000	+1.000
Tax on rent	–	–0.300	–0.300	–0.300	–0.300	–0.300
Net cash flow	–20.000	+0.700	+0.700	+0.700	+0.700	+27.465
Discount factor, 9.3%	1.000	0.915	0.837	0.766	0.701	0.641
Discounted cash flow	–20.000	+0.641	+0.586	+0.536	+0.491	+17.605
Base case NPV =	–0.141					

assume that the issue will take place shortly, and that tax relief is immediate, so no discounting is necessary.

Interest tax shield

The investment would contribute an increased borrowing capacity of £14m. The company's borrowing rate is 7%, so the notional interest payable is £980,000 per annum, which at a 30% tax rate would attract annual tax relief of £294,000. The present value of this tax relief is found by discounting over the five-year period of the loan:

Annual tax relief	£294,000
Present value of £1 per annum over 5 years at 7%	4.10
Present value of tax relief	£1,205,400

The discount rate used to value the tax relief is the nominal/pre-tax rate of interest on the loan. The relatively low rate reflects the security of this benefit.

The final stage is to add up the present values of the three components.

Adjusted Present Value

	£m
Base case NPV	–0.141
PV of issue expenses	–0.359
PV of tax shield	+1.205
APV	+0.705

Overall, the positive APV signifies that the investment is profitable, but only by virtue of the tax shield. Assessed in isolation from its financing implications, the investment looks unprofitable, and the issue costs increase this unprofitability, but the value of the tax shield more than compensates for these losses, resulting in an expected surplus overall.

In order to calculate an NPV in the example above using a risk-adjusted WACC as the discount rate, the expense of the equity issue, the benefit of the debt capacity and the risk would all need to be reflected appropriately in the discount rate. However, by valuing the investment separately from its funding implications, the APV method has the advantage of objectivity, clarity and, perhaps, accuracy.

In the section entitled 'The Weighted Average Cost of Capital' on page 111, the conclusion was reached that an investment should be appraised, not by reference to the cost of its actual funding, but to the company's WACC. This conclusion does not conflict with the APV method, because the APV reflects the funding *implications* of the investment, not its actual funding. In the example above, an implication of the decision is the increased borrowing capacity, although that capacity is not being used to fund the acquisition.

THE CAPM APPROACH: CONCLUSION

The principal advantage of the CAPM is that it provides an objective means of assessing risk. However, there are good theoretical and practical reasons to be cautious about its application. The model is based on the assumption of a 'perfect market' in which, for example, there is free information, no taxation and no transaction costs. Yet, it is proposed to apply it to the property market, a very imperfect market.

Another issue is that the CAPM is a single-period model, yet the very nature of DCF analysis is multi-period. There seems to be a consensus that applying the model to a multi-period context should not introduce substantial error. However, when applying the model to the five-year time-scale of Example 7.5, strictly speaking, we should have identified the redemption yield of five-year gilts as the risk-free return, beta should measure market risk over five-year holding periods, and the equity risk premium should be the excess return earned by equities over that of five-year gilts measured over five-year holding periods.

Another concern is that company betas are not stable and, inevitably, a beta derived from historic stock market performance may not reflect accurately on future risk. Similarly, the equity risk premium relevant to the future cannot reliably be identified from the past. However, in applying the CAPM to estimate a company's cost of capital, the crucial issue is whether betas provide a reasonable indication of companies' *relative* risk. Increasing use of the CAPM for this purpose suggests growing confidence in the model.

In applying the CAPM to property appraisal, there are good reasons to be doubly cautious. First, are betas measured over relatively short periods relevant to the long-term time horizons of most property investors? Second, there is the difficulty of identifying the betas appropriate to individual investments or development projects from the betas of property companies. But third, and fundamental, is that the application of the CAPM assumes that the only risk that matters to the investor is market-related risk. That would only hold true if the investor's portfolio is fully diversified and all specific risk had been eradicated. That might be acceptable in the case of institutional investors with large diversified portfolios, but highly improbable in the case of a property company. If the investor is not well diversified, the beta will understate the risk taken on.

All in all, it would seem unwise to rely on the CAPM to reflect risk reliably in property appraisal. None the less, it provides an objective alternative to the subjective assessment of risk reflected in a risk-adjusted WACC. Ultimately, appraisal involves judgement, art as well as science, and a sound judgement needs to be informed by examining a problem from different perspectives. That is why these matters have been investigated here.

SUMMARY

This chapter has examined the required return of both institutional and corporate investors. In all cases, the required return should be considered as an opportunity cost; that is, the return expected from an alternative investment of similar risk and other characteristics to the subject of the appraisal. In the case of institutional investors, the required return is normally assessed by adding a premium to the redemption yield of gilts. But in the case of companies, conventionally it is based on the after-tax weighted-average cost of capital (WACC). This method is well known and relatively simple. However, assessment of a risk-adjusted WACC depends on judgements about the company's cost of equity, optimal gearing and the investment's risk relative to the company. None of these can be quantified precisely, and the required return is inevitably a subjective assessment.

Some of the subjectivity can be avoided by a CAPM approach to appraisal, particularly if the APV method is used. That is more objective and sophisticated than an appraisal based on the WACC, requiring information about the funding of the investment in question. However, although the CAPM seems to be gaining credence in the business world, its practicability and reliability in property appraisal is unproven.

SELF-ASSESSMENT QUESTIONS

7.1 Estimate Company D's after-tax cost of equity capital from the following information:

Current share price: £1.50;
Annual dividend, to be paid shortly: 4 pence; and
Expected long term average dividend growth: 7% per annum.

7.2 Calculate the current after-tax cost of the debt capital issues of the following companies. Assume interest is paid annually in arrears and corporation tax is 30%:

(a) Company E issued 4% irredeemable debentures many years ago which are currently priced at £60 per £100 nominal (ex. div.).
(b) Company F has issued 7% debentures redeemable at par in three years. The current market price is £102 (ex. div.).
(c) Company G's 6.5% debentures are also redeemable in three years, but their price is currently £100 per £100 nominal (ex. div).

7.3 Estimate the return that a pension fund would require to justify a purchase of the Birches Mall (see Examples 6.3 on page 84 and 7.2 on page 112). Assume that the gross redemption yield on long-dated gilts is currently 5%.

7.4 Refer to Question 6.4, together with the following information about United Commercial Properties plc (UCP).

UCP is a substantial property company with a stock exchange listing. Its shares are currently priced at £6.50 and the annual dividend of 20 pence has recently been paid. The company's stockbrokers have recently predicted steady growth for profits, dividends and net assets of 6% per annum into the foreseeable future. The company's bonds are yielding 6.6%, and the gearing ratio is 20% (debt:debt+equity), which is felt to be somewhat on the low side. If UCP buys Toll Junction, it will fund the acquisition from liquid capital reserves.

UCP is a well-diversified property investment company holding good quality retail, office and industrial property.

Estimate UCP's target return for the purchase of Toll Junction Industrial Estate, and advise the company whether to buy the property at the asking price.

7.5 City Centres plc is considering the purchase of a multi-tenanted shopping centre expected to cost £25m, including expenses. The centre is expected to provide a rental income of £2.0m in Year 1 net of outgoings, and best estimates suggest that net rental income, rental value and capital value will all grow at an average rate of 5% per annum in the foreseeable future. For simplicity, assume a five-year holding period, rent received annually in arrears and no capital gains tax, depreciation allowances or expenses of sale.

The shopping centre is considered to be typical of investments held by the seller, Retail Estates plc, a company specialising in shopping centre investments. Retail Estates has a beta of 1.25 and a gearing ratio of 35% (debt:debt+equity).

It is estimated that the new investment would increase City Centres' borrowing capacity by £15m. However, the acquisition would be financed 50% by the company's retained equity and 50% by a new long-dated fixed interest bond issue paying 6% (gross). The costs of the issue are estimated at 1% of the capital raised (assume to be net of any tax allowances). City Centres pays tax at 30%.

Advise City Centres plc whether to buy the investment or not, using the APV method. Assume a risk-free rate of 5% and a forward market risk premium of 6%.

ANSWERS TO SELF-ASSESSMENT QUESTIONS

7.1 The cost of equity can be considered as the prospective dividend yield (based on the expected dividend payable in a year's time), plus the expected dividend growth rate. However, in this case, this year's dividend is about to be paid and the share price will be inflated by that amount. In the jargon, the share price is *cum.div.*, not *ex.div.* Therefore, this year's dividend should be stripped out of the price, and the prospective dividend yield based on the *ex.div.* price, as follows:

$$\left[\frac{4(1 + 0.07) \times 100}{150 - 4}\right] + 7\% = 9.93\%$$

Remember that appraisals should be undertaken after corporation tax but before personal taxes (to be paid by the shareholder). Dividends are paid out of net earnings after corporation tax has been levied, so no further tax is payable by the company, and no adjustment needs to be made in calculating the cost of equity.

7.2 *Company E*

$$\text{After-tax cost of debt} = \frac{4(1 - 0.3)}{60} = 4.67\%$$

Company F

The after-tax cost of debt is the IRR of the following cash flow.

			£
Year 0			+102.00
Year 1	–7.00 (1 – 0.3)		–4.90
Year 2	–7.00 (1 – 0.3)		–4.90
Year 3	–7.00 (1 – 0.3)	–4.90	
		–100.00	
			–104.90

IRR = 4.18% (after-tax cost of debt).

Company G

$$\text{After-tax cost of debt} = \frac{6.50(1 - 0.3)}{100} = 4.55\%$$

7.3 The target return would comprise the gilt yield (as the opportunity cost of relatively riskless capital) plus a yield premium of, say, 3%, as the property appears to be a good-quality investment. That suggests a target return of 8% per annum; no tax adjustment should be made, because pension funds are tax exempt.

7.4 Estimated cost of equity

$$= \left[\frac{20(1 + 0.06) \times 100}{650}\right] + 6\% = 9.26\%$$

Estimated cost of debt = 6.6 (1 – 0.3) = 4.62%.

WACC, at assumed optimal gearing ratio of 25%,
(0.75 × 9.26%) + (0.25 × 4.62%) = 8.1%.

Risk adjustment and target return

Toll Junction, as a small industrial estate, appears to be a relatively risky acquisition for a substantial property company with a well-diversified portfolio which includes shops and offices. A risk premium of, say, 1.9% might be added to the WACC to give a target return of 10%.

Decision

As the target return is well above the expected return of 6.9%, the purchase should be rejected.

7.5 First, find the asset beta of the shopping centre. It is typical of the assets held by Retail Estates, therefore we can estimate the property's beta, stripping out the effect of Retail Estates' gearing:

$$ß_{assets} = ß_{equity} \times \frac{V_e}{V_e + V_d\,(1 - T)}$$

$$= 1.25 \times \frac{65}{65 + 35(1 - 0.3)}$$

$$= 0.91.$$

Now calculate the after-tax required return using the CAPM:

$$r = r_f + ß\,(Er_m - r_f)$$
$$= 5.0\% + (0.91 \times 6\%)$$
$$= 10.46\%.$$

This is the target return (hurdle rate), assuming that the investment is to be funded by equity capital alone, and is the appropriate discount rate with which to calculate the base-case NPV.

Now set out the expected after-tax cash flow over the five-year period of ownership and calculate the base-case NPV (see Table 7.6).

Table 7.6 SAQ 7.5: Shopping centre

	Expected cash flows (£m) *Year*					
	0	*1*	*2*	*3*	*4*	*5*
Purchase and sale	−25.0	–	–	–	–	+31.91
Rental income	–	+2.00	+2.10	+2.21	+2.32	+2.43
Tax on rent	–	−0.60	−0.63	−0.66	−0.70	−0.73
After-tax cash flow	−25.0	+1.40	+1.47	+1.55	+1.62	+33.61

Base-case NPV @ 10.46% = +£0.149m.

Find the PV of the tax shield provided by the proposal. This needs to be based on the *borrowing capacity* introduced by the acquisition of the property (£15m) and not merely the amount being borrowed (£12.5m), because the surplus borrowing capacity will allow the company to raise further (relatively cheap) debt for a future project, if required.

Annual interest payments: 6% on £15m	£900,000
Annual tax relief at 30% tax	£270,000
PV of £1 per annum over 5 years at 6%	4.212
Present value of tax shield	£1,137,240

Now calculate the expenses of the bond issue. We need to include the cost of the total issue of £12.5m because the issue is a consequence of making the buy decision.

In order to raise the £12.5m net of issue costs of 1%, £12.626m needs to be raised. The costs of £0.126m are deemed to be immediate, and hence are a present value (negative). Therefore, the APV is as follows:

		£m
Base-case NPV	=	+0.149
PV of tax shield	=	+1.137
PV of issue costs	=	−0.126
APV	=	+1.160

The positive APV means that the investment should be bought.

8

Short-cut DCF

OVERVIEW

Having dealt with most of the theoretical underpinning of cash-flow appraisal, the next two chapters illustrate its application to various special situations in property investment. In this chapter, we examine 'short-cut' DCF, a simplified form of analysis which, none the less, supports a large amount of day-to-day market analysis and decision-making in property investment. It also presents an opportunity to expand on the issue of depreciation in property appraisal.

THE RELATIONSHIP BETWEEN RETURN, GROWTH, YIELD AND RENT REVIEW

As explained in Chapter 2, the market price of any income-earning investment can be considered as the present value of the expected income flow to be generated by the investment. In the simplified case, of:

- a freehold property investment;
- just let on a perpetual lease at its current rental value (R_o);
- subject to rent review to rental value every three years;
- with rental value growth constant in perpetuity; and
- rent paid annually in arrears,

the market price can be represented as follows:

$$P_0 = \frac{R_0}{(1+r)} + \frac{R_0}{(1+r)^2} + \frac{R_0}{(1+r)^3} + \frac{R_0\,(1+g)^3}{(1+r)^4} + \ldots\ldots\ldots \qquad (8.1)$$

where g = investors' expected rental value growth rate per annum;
P_0 = current market price or value; and
r = investors' target return per annum.

Substituting, $y = \frac{R_0}{P_0}$ (current rental yield of rack-rented freehold property)

and, n = period (years) between rent reviews,

Equation (8.1) reduces to:

$$y = r - r\left(\frac{(1 + g)^n - 1}{(1 + r)^n - 1}\right) \tag{8.2}$$

This equation defines the relationship (under the simplifying assumptions) between:

- the rental yield of a rack-rented freehold property (y);
- investors' target return per annum (IRR) (r);
- investors' expected rental growth rate per annum (g); and
- the period between rent reviews (years) (n).

Solving Equation (8.2) for y will find the rental yield that is consistent with a certain target return, growth rate and rent review period.

The equation can be restated in terms of the rental growth rate (g), as follows:

$$g = \left(\frac{(r - y)(1 + r)^n + y}{r}\right)^{1/n} - 1 \tag{8.3}$$

Solving Equation (8.3) for g will find the rental value growth rate per annum that is consistent with a certain yield, target return and rent review period. The relationship cannot be restated simply in terms of r. That is why we have to calculate an IRR by iteration.

Equations (8.2) and (8.3) are the equivalent for property of the relationship between the dividend yield (d), target return (r) and dividend growth rate (g_d) for equity shares, which derives from the dividend discount model. On similar assumptions about constant dividend growth and dividend payments being annual in arrears, the comparable relationships are:

$$d = r - g_d \tag{8.4}$$

$$g_d = r - d \tag{8.5}$$

The only reason for the greater complexity of Equations (8.2) and (8.3) is that, under normal commercial property leases in Britain, rent cannot vary annually. Typically, rent is fixed for five-year periods. In the event of a lease being subject to annual rent reviews, the relationships would be:

$$y = r - g \tag{8.6}$$

$$g = r - y \tag{8.7}$$

Despite the reality that rent is not normally paid annually in arrears, leases are not perpetual and rental growth fluctuates in cycles, Equations (8.2) and (8.3) provide a useful basis for decision-making without employing a full DCF analysis. The growth variable is best considered as an *average* growth rate; in fact, an average influenced by the time value of money. Growth expected soon is more valuable than the same growth later on. This 'short-cut' analysis is particularly relevant to the perspective of long-term investors, such as life assurance and pension funds, and to the sectors of the market dominated by them. In Britain, these institutions typically buy high-quality properties subject to long leases, regular rent reviews and let to reliable tenants on strong repairing and insuring (FRI) covenants. Traditionally, they have taken a long-term and passive view of their investments. From this perspective, the simplified assumptions of the analysis are acceptable.

From the perspective of investing institutions, the redemption yield on long-dated gilts provides a particularly relevant measure of the opportunity cost of capital, because of the long-term nature of the liabilities of such funds, and the important role that gilts play in their multi-asset portfolios. Therefore, these funds will perceive property's risk as its risk *relative* to bonds and equities in the *portfolio context*. The low correlation of property's returns with both gilts and equities, and property's record as a hedge against inflation, are qualities that make property attractive to institutional funds. By contrast, its poor liquidity, management burden and lack of price transparency tend to detract.

The application of these equations is best illustrated by examples.

Example 8.1

High-quality shops let on long FRI leases subject to five-year rent reviews are currently yielding 6%. Can such investments be justified for investors who expect rental value growth to average 3% per annum into the foreseeable future, and whose target return is 8% per annum?

The question can be answered in three ways:

- By finding the required yield and comparing it with the yield available (Method 1);

- By finding the growth rate required and comparing it with the growth expected (Method 2); or
- By finding the expected IRR and comparing it with the target IRR (Method 3).

Clearly, it is only necessary to answer the question in one way, but here all three methods are illustrated, to demonstrate the alternatives.

Method 1
Find the rental yield required to justify the investment, on the assumption of 3% growth and an 8% target return, and compare with the yield available:

$$y = r - r\left(\frac{(1+g)^n - 1}{(1+r)^n - 1}\right)$$

$$y = 0.08 - 0.08\left(\frac{(1+0.03)^5 - 1}{(1+0.08)^5 - 1}\right)$$

$$y = 0.08 - 0.08\left(\frac{0.1593}{0.4693}\right)$$

$$y = 0.08 - 0.0272$$

$$y = 0.0528, \textit{ say}, 5.3\%$$

Note, from the penultimate line above, that the effect of the right-hand side of the formula is to reduce 3% *rental value growth* per annum to 2.72% average *income growth*, because the rent is fixed within each five-year period.

A 5.3% yield is required to give investors an 8% return, assuming 3% rental growth. A yield of 6% is available. So, the investment is justified.

Method 2
Find the rental growth rate required to justify the investment on the assumption of an 8% target return, and compare with the growth rate expected:

$$g = \left(\frac{(r-y)(1+r)^n + y}{r}\right)^{1/n} - 1$$

$$g = \left(\frac{(0.08-0.06)(1+0.08)^5 + 0.06}{0.08}\right)^{1/5} - 1$$

$$g = (1.11733)^{1/5} - 1$$

$$g = 0.0224, \textit{ say}, 2.2\%$$

A 2.2% growth rate per annum is required to give investors an 8% return; 3% growth is expected. So, the investment is justified.

Method 3

Find the return expected on the assumption of 3% growth per annum, and compare with the target return.

Here, we cannot employ a simple algebraic equation, so we need to calculate the expected IRR by iteration. We shall assume an investment price of £1m.

In estimating the relevant cash flow, it is simplest and sufficient in this case to assume a sale of the property at the date of the first rent review. The notional sale price will reflect the investment's perpetual nature, and the cash flow fully encapsulates the effect of growth and the rent review period. In this simple example, no greater accuracy will be gained from extending the cash flows to subsequent rent reviews, provided that the assumption of constant rental growth in perpetuity is replaced by an assumption that the property's yield remains constant. On that assumption, rental value growth over the first five years must be converted into capital growth at the date of the rent review. Hence, the notional sale price of the property in Year 5 is:

$$£1.0\text{m } (1 + 0.03)^5 = £1.159\text{m}$$

The price of £1.159m is reflecting both the growth achieved in the first five years and acting as a surrogate for the assumption of further rental growth into perpetuity. The expected cash flow is shown in Table 8.1.

The expected IRR is 8.67%, and the required IRR is 8%, so the investment is justified.

Necessarily, the three methods arrive at the same answer. Note that, if the property had been let on annual rent reviews, the expected IRR would

Table 8.1 Example 8.1: expected cash flow (£m)

	Years	
0	*1–5*	*5*
–1.0	+0.06	+1.159

Expected IRR = 8.67% per annum (by calculator)

have been 9% ($y + g$). The effect of five-yearly reviews is to reduce the investor's return by just 0.33% per annum.

This example has illustrated a simple application of the use of the equations in investment analysis. The calculations have been made on a before-tax basis, and buying and selling costs ignored, which is conventional for this type of analysis.

As illustrated in Example 8.1, short-cut DCF can be used as a simple rule-of-thumb form of analysis to assist investment decision-making. It is a means of disaggregating and making explicit what is implicit in market prices and yields, enabling judgements to be made about whether property prices are relatively expensive or cheap. For example, the implicit growth expectation revealed by the analysis can be compared with growth forecasts based on economic prospects; or expected returns can be compared with returns available from alternative investments such as government bonds.

If the rent review period is assumed to be a constant, Equation (8.2) illustrates that property yields (and prices) vary in response to changes in investors' target returns and their growth expectations. However, both of these variables can be subdivided into two components. The target return comprises a cost of capital component and a yield premium to reflect relative risk and liquidity. The growth variable is determined by market growth trends as well as by the impact of depreciation on buildings (see page 137). Arguably, therefore, four variables determine property yields.

THE MARKET'S IMPLIED GROWTH EXPECTATION

We shall now examine in more detail the growth variable, g, as calculated from Equation (8.3) above.

If, as indicated in Example 8.1, shops are yielding 6% and investors require an 8% return on such investments, then it follows that implicitly they must be expecting 2.2% per annum growth, assuming that investors are rational, and that the property market is 'efficient' – that is, market prices respond quickly to investors' changing expectations and requirements through the forces of supply and demand.

If investors (collectively) were anticipating higher growth than 2.2%, then prices would rise and yields would fall below 6%. If investors anticipated growth lower than 2.2%, prices would fall, and yields rise. So (again assuming an 8% target return), investors must implicitly be expecting 2.2% growth. That is why we call this growth variable the market's implied growth expectation (MIGE). It can never be measured precisely because the consensus target return of investors can never be identified precisely, but the target return can be estimated with sufficient confidence to enable a sensible estimate of the MIGE to be made.

On the assumption of perpetual investment or constant yields, the MIGE must represent the market's expectation of rental value growth. However, the market may sometimes be anticipating changing yields, in which case the MIGE will incorporate expected capital gain or loss arising from changing yields as well as from changing rental values. Notionally, the MIGE is a constant growth rate but, as discussed above, it is best considered as a long-term *average* expected growth rate.

DEPRECIATION THROUGH OBSOLESCENCE

The MIGE derived by Equation (8.3) is a growth expectation as reduced by investors' expectation of depreciation. This is because the prices that investors are prepared to pay for property must reflect their expectation for depreciation. Hence, depreciation must be reflected in property yields and, as the MIGE is derived from yields, the MIGE must reflect the consensus expectation of those investors active in the relevant sector (high-quality shops in Example 8.1).

Depreciation of property through the obsolescence of buildings is of great significance to investment performance and to investment decisions, and it is important to be clear in what way it is being allowed for in an investment appraisal. If a decision is being based on an analysis similar to Method 2 in Example 8.1, it is important that the required growth and expected growth are being compared on the same basis (net of depreciation, in that case).

By measuring value change of hypothetical modern property in Britain, the CB Hillier Parker Rent Index excludes the impact of depreciation. So, if, in an appraisal, future rental growth estimates are based on Hillier Parker data, depreciation will not be included and the growth estimates will not be compatible with the MIGE.

Rental value growth arising from market forces and the impact of depreciation on the individual property interact to determine the growth rate of the individual property. The correct relationship between growth on hypothetical property and on actual property subject to depreciation is as follows:

$$g_i = (1 + g_m)(1 - d_p) - 1 \qquad (8.8)$$

where

g_i = the growth rate per annum of an individual property subject to depreciation;

g_m = the growth rate per annum of comparable but hypothetical perpetually modern property; and

d_p = the rate of depreciation per annum.

Example 8.2

Assuming an average annual rate of depreciation of 2½% per annum, what would be the expected growth rate of an office block if the growth rate for hypothetical brand-new equivalents is expected to average 7% per annum?

$$g_i = (1 + g_m)(1 - d_p) - 1$$

$$g_i = (1 + 0.07)(1 - 0.025) - 1$$

$$g_i = 0.043$$

The outcome, 4.3%, is not substantially different from simply deducting the expected rate of depreciation from the growth rate before depreciation (4.5% in this case). In most circumstances that would be sufficient, particularly in view of the fact that both growth and depreciation are impossible to forecast accurately.

The MIGE derived from a property's yield will reflect the market's expectation for depreciation, acting to reduce rental growth and raise the property's yield. But the market's expectation can prove unreliable, as in the 1980s and 1990s, when the advent of computers into most office-based functions rendered obsolete much older office space. The rate of depreciation through obsolescence is not easily predictable. It varies according to property type, age of building and over different periods in time. However, like rental growth, it is an imponderable which needs to be taken into account in appraisal, either by making explicit allowance for future repair or refurbishment, or as a drag on rental growth, or as a reduction to the notional terminal value on sale, or perhaps in all three ways, as long as that does not result in double (or triple) counting.

OTHER APPLICATIONS

The two Equations (8.2) and (8.3) have various potential applications both to the analysis of the real estate market and to making decisions about individual investments. Equation (8.2) can be used to indicate the likely impact of changing rates of growth or depreciation, gilt yields or yield premiums. The equation can help to explain different yields between properties as well as changing yields over time. Some applications are illustrated in the questions at the end of this chapter.

Here, we shall end with an example to illustrate the impact of different rent review periods on required yields and rents.

Example 8.3

You are acting for the owner of a vacant factory worth £1m, which you are confident you can let on a long lease at £100,000 per annum FRI, subject to five-year rent reviews. A good potential tenant is unwilling to agree to five-year rent reviews, but would accept seven-year reviews. What rent should you charge on a seven-year review basis to equal the return expected on the five-year review basis? Assume expected growth (net of depreciation) is 3½% per annum.

(1) Find the expected IRR on a five-year review basis.
Notional sale price at date of first rent review:

$$= £1.0\ (1 + 0.035)^5 = £1.188\text{m}$$

The expected cash flow and IRR are shown in Table 8.2.

(2) Find the initial yield required on a seven-year review basis to equal the IRR expected on the five-year review basis:

$$y = r - r\left(\frac{(1 + g)^n - 1}{(1 + r)^n - 1}\right)$$

$$y = 0.1291 - 0.1291\left(\frac{(1 + 0.035)^7 - 1}{(1 + 0.1291)^7 - 1}\right)$$

$$y = 0.10286$$

Therefore, on a seven-year review basis, a rent of £102,860 would be needed to provide the same annual return as expected by a rent of £100,000 per annum on a five-year review basis (assuming 3½% growth per annum).

Table 8.2 Example 8.3: expected cash flow (£m)

	Years	
0	*1–5*	*5*
−1.0	+0.1	+1.188

Expected IRR = 12.91% per annum (by calculator)

The calculation above assumes that the proposed lease is perpetual. A full DCF would be needed to take precise account of the impact of, say, a 20-year lease, after which the review period might revert to five years.

SUMMARY

This chapter has examined the relationship between the four principal variables that explain market prices and investment returns from property: namely, the rental yield, growth rate, target return and rent review period. The impact on growth of depreciation from obsolescence has also been investigated, and illustrations given of simple analyses that can be undertaken using the formulae defining these relationships.

SELF-ASSESSMENT QUESTIONS

8.1 High-quality industrial investments let on long FRI leases subject to five-year reviews are currently providing yields of 7%. Do you believe this yield is sufficient, assuming future rental growth averaging 2% net of depreciation? Government bonds are currently providing gross redemption yields of around 5.5%, and investors require a risk premium of 3.5%.

8.2 High-quality retail investments let on long FRI leases subject to five-year reviews yield 5%, while long-dated government bonds yield 6½%. What changes in retail property yield would you anticipate if a sharp decline in expectations for future inflation caused both a 1½% fall in bond yields and a 1% fall in future rental growth? Assume a yield premium of 3% in this case.

8.3 Yields of 6% on city centre offices are assumed to reflect a target return of 9.8% (comprising a 6.5% bond yield + 3.3% risk premium) and growth of 4.3% (comprising 7% growth for modern properties less 2.5% depreciation – see Example 8.2, page 138). What might be the impact on yields of a growing concern about the rate of obsolescence which increased *both* the required risk premium and the expected rate of depreciation by 0.5% for each?

ANSWERS TO SELF-ASSESSMENT QUESTIONS

8.1 Find the yield required and compare with the yield available.

Target return = 5.5 + 3.5 = 9.0%

$$y = r - r\left(\frac{(1+g)^n - 1}{(1+r)^n - 1}\right)$$

$$y = 0.09 - 0.09\left(\frac{(1+0.02)^5 - 1}{(1+0.09)^5 - 1}\right)$$

$$y = 0.073, \text{ or } 7.3\%$$

The yield required (7.3%) is more than the yield available (7%), so the investment is not justified on the assumptions made. In fact, the calculation was hardly necessary. If the properties had been let on annual rent reviews, the expected IRR (7% + 2%) would have equalled the target IRR (5.5% + 3.5%). Hence, with five-year reviews, the expected return and yield available must be insufficient.

This question could also be answered by comparing the growth implied by the yield with the growth expected, or by comparing the return expected with the target return, as shown in Example 8.1 (see pages 133–6).

8.2 In order to identify the yield required by investors under the new circumstances, we first need to identify the current implied growth expectation:

$$g = \left(\frac{(r-y)(1+r)^n + y}{r}\right)^{1/n} - 1$$

$$g = \left(\frac{(0.095 - 0.05)(1+0.095)^5 + 0.05}{0.095}\right)^{1/5} - 1$$

$$g = (1.2720)^{1/5} - 1$$

$$g = 0.0493, \text{ or } 4.93\%$$

If 4.93% is the current growth expectation, then the new growth expectation would be 3.93%. We can now calculate the yield that is consistent with that growth rate and the lower target return:

$$y = r - r\left(\frac{(1+g)^n - 1}{(1+r)^n - 1}\right)$$

$$y = 0.08 - 0.08\left(\frac{(1 + 0.0393)^5 - 1}{(1 + 0.08)^5 - 1}\right)$$

y = 0.0438, *or* 4.4%

The retail yield would tend to fall to 4.4%.

8.3 First, calculate the impact on the expected growth rate of the higher rate of depreciation:

$$g_i = (1 + g_m)(1 - d_p) - 1$$
$$g_i = (1 + 0.07)(1 - 0.03) - 1$$
$$g_i = 0.038$$

Now calculate the required yield based on the lower growth and higher target return:

$$y = r - r\left(\frac{(1 + g)^n - 1}{(1 + r)^n - 1}\right)$$

$$y = 0.103 - 0.103\left(\frac{(1 + 0.038)^5 - 1}{(1 + 0.103)^5 - 1}\right)$$

y = 0.0696, *or* 7%

Yields would tend to rise to 7%. In fact, the calculation was hardly necessary. If investors' required return rises by 0.5% and the expected growth rate falls by 0.5% because of increased depreciation, then the initial yield must tend to rise by about 1%.

9

Buy or Lease, and Leaseback Decisions

OVERVIEW

Up to now, this book has been concerned primarily with decisions about projects or portfolio investments. In this chapter, we examine decisions that face corporate occupiers of commercial real estate – whether to buy or lease property, and whether to raise capital by sale and leaseback. No new concepts or principles are involved. It is primarily a case of applying the principles and techniques developed in earlier chapters to the perspective of the occupier.

THE BUY OR LEASE DECISION

The decision whether to buy property as an owner-occupier or lease as a tenant faces both private individuals acquiring a home and businesses acquiring commercial property. In each case, there will be many subjective and unquantifiable factors to be taken into account, and in all cases the decision should be a judgement by the decision-maker, rather than the outcome of a calculation. Yet a judgement, even an intuitive judgement, will be helped by a calculation that captures the quantifiable costs and benefits that arise as a result of the decision.

As the relevant principles have already been introduced in earlier chapters, we shall proceed here using examples. Example 9.1 concerns the acquisition of a computer system. This provides a relatively simple context in which to introduce the concept of the buy or lease decision before we proceed to the more complex situation of real estate.

Example 9.1

Reliant Agency plc needs to acquire a new computer system. After extensive investigations of alternatives available, it is convinced that the system available from Ace Computers provides the best value for its needs. The system is expected to have a five-year life and no residual value.

Ace offers two methods of acquisition to Reliant Agency. It can buy the whole system outright for £100,000, or lease it for £35,000 per annum (paid annually in advance) for three years, plus £20,000 per annum for the next two years. Ace Computers would guarantee the necessary service of the system under either deal. Which method of acquisition would you recommend?

Assume that a first-year allowance of 40% and 25% writing-down allowances against tax are available to Reliant under the buy option, and that tax relief is available at 30% on rental payments under the lease option, received at the end of the year. Also assume that, under the buy option, Reliant elects to treat the computer system as a short-life asset. This allows the system to be 'de-pooled' from the company's other plant and machinery, and provides the benefit of a balancing allowance on disposal within a five-year period.

Because of the near-certainty of the cash flows, a low-risk cost of capital of 8% is adopted as Reliant's required return.

Answer

Essentially, the procedure is to compare the after-tax cash flows that would result from either the buy or the lease decision. Either the NPV or IRR method can be used. Both are illustrated here. The tax implications of the decision are crucial and must be incorporated into the cash flows.

First, calculate the value of the plant and machinery allowances available under the buy option; see Table 9.1. The tax relief is the reduction in corporation tax which would otherwise be payable, assuming that Reliant Agency is making taxable profits from its business activity. The tax relief is a change in cash flow which arises as a result of the decision to buy the computer. It must therefore be included in the DCF calculation.

Second, calculate the NPV of the Buy Option; see Table 9.2.

Third, calculate the NPV of the Lease Option; see Table 9.3.

The NPV cost of the buy option is significantly less than that of the lease option. So, the buy option is preferred.

An alternative to comparing the NPVs of the options is *incremental analysis;* that is, to calculate the IRR of the extra cost of the initially more expensive option and compare it with the required return. This form of analysis was introduced in Chapter 4 (see page 46). This time we shall lay out the net cash flows from our example horizontally and deduct the lease cash flow from the buy cash flow to get the incremental cash flow as shown in Table 9.4.

Table 9.1 Value of taxation allowances, buy option

		Tax relief @ 30%	
	£	£	
Cost of system	100,000		
40% FYA	40,000	12,000	Year 1
	60,000		
25% WDA	15,000	4,500	Year 2
	45,000		
25% WDA	11 250	3,375	Year 3
	33,750		
25% WDA	8,438	2,531	Year 4
	25,312		
Scrap value	–		
Balancing allowance	25,312	7,594	Year 5

Table 9.2 NPV of buy option

Year	*Outlay (£)*	*Tax relief (£)*	*Discount factor @ 8%*	*Present value @ 8% (£)*
0	–100,000		1.000	–100,000.00
1		+12,000	0.926	+11,112.00
2		+4,500	0.857	+3,856.50
3		+3,375	0.794	+2,679.75
4		+2,531	0.735	+1,860.29
5		+7,594	0.681	+5,171.51
				NPV @ 8% –75,319.95

As the IRR of the incremental cash flow (21.6% per annum) exceeds the required return (8% per annum), the initially more expensive option should be selected – that is, the buy option. The incremental IRR method selects the same option as the NPV method.

The concept represented by the incremental cash flow in Table 9.4 is that, by spending £65,000 extra in Year 0 to buy the computer system, the company would gain extra benefits of £36,500 in Year 1, £29,000

Table 9.3 NPV of lease option

Year	*Rent (£)*	*Tax relief @ 30% (£)*	*Net cash flow (£)*	*Discount factor @ 8%*	*Present value @ 8% (£)*
0	–35,000	–	–35,000	1.000	–35,000.00
1	–35,000	+10,500	–24,500	0.926	–22,687.00
2	–35,000	+10,500	–24,500	0.857	–20,996.50
3	–20,000	+10,500	–9,500	0.794	–7,543.00
4	–20,000	+6,000	–14,000	0.735	–10,290.00
5		+6,000	+6,000	0.681	+4,086.00
				NPV @ 8%	–92,430.50

Table 9.4 Incremental cash flows (£), buy and lease options

Option	*Year*					
	0	*1*	*2*	*3*	*4*	*5*
Buy	–100,000	+12,000	+4,500	+3,375	+2,531	+7,594
Lease	–35,000	–24,500	–24,500	–9,500	–14,000	+6,000
Incremental CF	–65,000	+36,500	+29,000	+12,875	+16,531	+1,594

Incremental IRR = 21.6% per annum (by calculator)

in Year 2 and so on. These benefits arise from avoiding the need to pay rent and from obtaining tax relief by depreciation allowances. The incremental IRR of 21.6% per annum measures these benefits as a return on the extra £65,000 cost. The incremental cash flow is not a real cash flow, but a measure of the net costs and benefits from selecting the buy option.

Note that the decision being made here is not whether to acquire a computer system. That decision has already been made by Reliant. The decision is to find the best method of acquisition – buy or lease, which are mutually exclusive alternatives.

Example 9.1 has identified the concepts underlying the buy or lease decision and the NPV and IRR solutions to the problem. However, the context was simple: all present and future costs and benefits were known. That is unlikely in the real estate context, where the decision is normally made for a longer time period and without certain knowledge of future costs and benefits. We shall examine these issues in Example 9.2.

Example 9.2

Beans & Broccoli plc is a vegetable processing business currently seeking new premises because of expansion. It has identified a suitable vacant property that is on the market for sale or to let. Beans & Broccoli needs advice on whether to buy or lease the property.

The price of the property is £1m. Under the lease option, the initial rent would be £100,000 per annum subject to a five-year rent review to rental value on a ten-year lease. The landlord would pay repairs and insurance.

Assume the following:

- Food processing is not an activity that qualifies the building for Industrial Buildings Allowances;
- Under both options, Beans & Broccoli would install the necessary plant and machinery, costing £200,000, and would gain the tax relief;
- The cost of annual building repairs and insurance is currently estimated at £4,000, and is expected to grow at 2.5% per annum;
- Best estimates suggest rental value growth averaging 3% per annum into the foreseeable future;
- Corporation tax is at 30%;
- Stamp duty and legal fees and expenses are 4% and 0.5% of the purchase price, respectively. Under the lease option, Beans & Broccoli would incur legal fees and expenses of £2,000. Assume fees and expenses of selling the property would be 3% of proceeds;
- Beans & Broccoli's WACC is 10%;
- All cash flows occur annually in arrears and tax relief is received in the same year as the cost is incurred; and
- There is a ten-year period of occupation under either option.

Answer

We need to identify cash flows that arise as a result of either option. However, cash flows that are the same for both options can be ignored, because they do not affect the decision. This is obvious in an incremental analysis. Identical cash flows that arise under both buy and lease options would be cancelled out in calculating the incremental cash flow. In this example, both the cost and tax relief arising from the plant and machinery will be identical for both options. Hence, this can be ignored.

In this case, the cost of building repairs and insurance cannot be ignored, because under the lease option it is paid by the landlord, but under the buy option Beans & Broccoli would have the responsibility as owner-occupier.

Estimated Cash Flow – Buy Option

Cost of purchase, Year 0
£1,000,000 (1 + 0.045) = £1,045,000.

Repairs and insurance (after tax)
Calculated as shown in Table 9.5.

Estimated sale proceeds, Year 10

Expected rental value, Year 10: £100,000 $(1 + 0.03)^{10}$	£134,392
Capitalise at 12% in perpetuity	8.333
	£1,119,889
Less: Sale fees and expenses, say 3%	£33,597
Estimated sale proceeds	£1,086,292

Although the rental growth rate used will reflect depreciation, the property's capitalisation yield in Year 10 is also likely to be affected. That is why 12% has been adopted as the estimated yield at the date of sale compared with the current (gross) yield of 10%.

No tax has been deducted from the small capital gain realised in Year 10, as Beans & Broccoli are likely to avoid (or postpone indefinitely) the tax by 'roll-over relief'. This refers to a provision that allows a company to postpone tax on a realised capital gain if the proceeds are reinvested in the business.

Table 9.5 Repairs and insurance (after tax)

Year		£
1	£4000 (1 + 0.025) (1 – 0.3)	2,870
2	£4000 $(1 + 0.025)^2$ (1 – 0.3)	2,942
3	£4000 $(1 + 0.025)^3$ (1 – 0.3)	3,015
4	£4000 $(1 + 0.025)^4$ (1 – 0.3)	3,091
5	£4000 $(1 + 0.025)^5$ (1 – 0.3)	3,168
6	£4000 $(1 + 0.025)^6$ (1 – 0.3)	3,247
7	£4000 $(1 + 0.025)^7$ (1 – 0.3)	3,328
8	£4000 $(1 + 0.025)^8$ (1 – 0.3)	3,412
9	£4000 $(1 + 0.025)^9$ (1 – 0.3)	3,497
10	£4000 $(1 + 0.025)^{10}$ (1 – 0.3)	3,584

Estimated rental payments (after tax), lease option

Years 1–5:	£100,000 (1 – 0.3)	£70,000
Years 6–10:	£100,000 $(1 + 0.03)^5$ (1 – 0.3)	£81,149

We now set out the estimated cash flows under the two options in Table 9.6.

The incremental IRR is the effective return that Beans & Broccoli expect on the £1.043m extra Year 0 cost of buying the property. That return is the net effect of avoiding rental payments, making a small capital gain, but having to pay repairs and insurance. However, the company's WACC is 10%, significantly greater than the incremental IRR, therefore buying the property would not appear to be sensible. The decision should be to lease. This is confirmed by the lower NPV cost of the lease option.

If, however, the incremental IRR in the example above had been higher, say 9%, the decision to buy or lease would have been less obvious. The target return applicable to any investment is only the same as the investor's WACC if the investment's risk is identical to the risk of the company. In this case, investing in the property may be significantly less risky than Beans & Broccoli, hence the appropriate target return should perhaps be less than the WACC, say 8% or 9%.

In logic, any decision can only be made by reference to alternatives. On the face of it, leasing a property may seem the less risky alternative, and

Table 9.6 Estimated cash flows, Beans & Broccoli

Year	*Buy and sell (£)*	*Repairs and insurance (£)*	*Buy option (£)*	*Lease option (£)*	*Incremental cash flow (£)*
0	–1,045,000	–	–1,045,000	–2,000	–1,043,000
1	–	–2,870	–2,870	–70,000	+67,130
2	–	–2,942	–2,942	–70,000	+67,058
3	–	–3,015	–3,015	–70,000	+66,985
4	–	–3,091	–3,091	–70,000	+66,909
5	–	–3,168	–3,168	–70,000	+66,832
6	–	–3,247	–3,247	–81,149	+77,902
7	–	–3,328	–3,328	–81,149	+77,737
8	–	–3,412	_3,412	–81,149	+77,737
9	–	–3,497	–3,497	–81,149	+77,652
10	+1,086,292	–3,584	+1,082,708	–81,149	+1,163,857
NPV of buy option @ 10%			–645,569		
NPV of lease option @ 10%				–458,362	
Incremental IRR					7.15% p.a.

avoids the need for capital. But leasing raises a company's effective gearing – the so-called operational gearing.

Financial gearing increases corporate risk, because interest payments and debt repayment are prior charges on company earnings. But rent due under a lease is also a prior charge, and unlike the cost of debt, it is not reduced by inflation (because of rent reviews). Therefore, by avoiding an increase in operational gearing, ownership rather than leasing property may be the safer alternative, perhaps justifying a target return below the WACC. However, there are many other factors that would influence the decision. Most of all, there is the greater flexibility of ownership – for example, to alter or extend the building as needed for the purposes of business, or to sell up and move to an alternative property or location. The long lease traditional in Britain, and constraints imposed under a lease, can be a disadvantage to companies in times of growth or change.

THE SALE AND LEASEBACK DECISION

The concept of sale and leaseback is simple. It usually involves the sale of the freehold interest in a property to an investor, on condition that the property is leased back to the original owner-occupier as tenant. Sometimes, however, a leasehold interest is sold on condition that the seller becomes the occupying sub-tenant.

Any type of property may be the subject of a sale and leaseback, but in Britain such deals are particularly popular in retail property of investment quality. The arrangement is attractive to property investors because, typically, it provides an investment with a reliable tenant on a long lease.

From the seller's perspective, the usual purpose of a sale and leaseback is to raise capital. It is an alternative to raising new debt or equity – for example, by market issues. But, rather than raising new capital, these deals *release* existing capital tied up in property.

Leasebacks are often driven by taxation. Owners who are unable to benefit fully from tax allowances (perhaps because their business is not making profits) may sell the property to investors looking to shelter profits against tax. The sale price can be relatively high (or the rent payable under the leaseback relatively low) because of such tax allowances.

The recommended analysis for sale and leaseback decisions is similar to that for the buy or lease decision. However, instead of calculating the effective return on the capital to be invested and comparing it with the cost, we calculate the cost of the capital to be raised by the sale and leaseback, and compare it with the cost of capital raised by other means. The question is not whether to invest in property but whether to disinvest, and the relevant comparison is between the cash flow arising from the sale and leaseback, and the cash flow arising from retaining the property. The procedure is best illustrated by an example.

In examining the buy or lease decision, we started from an assumption that the company had a profitable use for the property, but needed to decide what was the best method of acquisition. In a sale and leaseback decision, there is a presumption that the owner has a profitable use for the property and the capital to be raised. The question is to find the best method of raising the capital.

Example 9.3

Fresco plc, a national food retailer, wants to raise £50m of long-term capital to finance expansion. Essentially, it has three options:

- Raise equity capital by rights issue;
- Raise debt capital by issuing bonds paying 7% per annum; or
- Sell several of its stores worth £50m, on condition of leaseback on a 25-year lease at an initial rent of £3.2m (rental value on FRI lease) subject to five-year reviews.

Calculate the cost to Fresco of these three methods of raising capital, and discuss their relative merits in the context of the company's gearing.

Assume:

- The company's shares have a prospective dividend yield of 3.5%, and dividend growth is expected to average 7% per annum into the foreseeable future;
- The retail stores are well-located and best estimates indicate future rental growth averaging 5.5% per annum;
- Corporation tax is 30%, payable in the same year as the liability arises;
- Under the leaseback option, Fresco would retain ownership of, and responsibility for, plant and machinery;
- If the sale and leaseback goes ahead, Fresco will incur fees and expenses of 1.5% of the sale proceeds;
- If the sale and leaseback goes ahead, no tax will be payable on capital gain realised due to roll-over relief; and
- Fresco's debt is currently 30% of capital employed.

Answer

Cost of equity capital by rights issue

Dividend yield + dividend growth + expenses

= 3.5% + 7% + (say) 0.3% = 10.8%.

Cost of debt capital by bond issue
Interest rate + issue expenses – tax relief
= (7.0% + (say) 0.1%) (1 – 0.3) = 4.97%, *say* 5%.

Cost of capital by sale and leaseback
As Fresco would be responsible for repairs and insurance to the properties both as owner-occupier and tenant, these would cancel out in an incremental analysis, and should be ignored. Similarly, as Fresco would retain ownership and responsibility for plant and machinery under the leaseback option, once again there would be no change in the company's liability to repair, or their benefit from tax relief. Thus, in this example the cash flow analysis is quite simple, consisting of capital realised, net-of-tax rental payments under the sale and leaseback option, and the expected value of the properties for sale in the future, if retained.

For simplicity, we shall adopt a 15-year period rather than the 25-year lease period. This will affect the outcome, but not substantially. As there is no reason to believe that a sale will actually take place at the end of the 15 years (under the retain option), no sale costs or any allowance for capital gains taxation will be made.

Sale proceeds under S & L option
50.0 (1 – 0.015) = £49.250m.

Estimated net rental payments under S & L option

Years 1–5	3.2 (1 – 0.3)	= £2.240m;
Years 6–10	$3.2\,(1 + 0.055)^{5}\,(1 - 0.3)$	= £2.928m;
Years 11–15	$3.2\,(1 + 0.055)^{10}\,(1 - 0.3)$	= £3.826m.

Expected capital value of properties, Year 15 (Retain option)
$50.0\,(1 + 0.055)^{15}$ = £111.624m.

By compounding the current value of the stores at the same growth rate as rental value, it is implied that the Year 15 yield on the properties will be the same as at present: if the yield remains unchanged, all rental growth must be converted to capital growth. This could (perhaps) be justified in the case of prime quality retail property where the bulk of value may be in the land (because of location) rather than in the building. Depreciation through obsolescence may be minor, and to some extent will be reflected in the rental growth rate.

The cash flows arising from the alternative options of retaining the properties or selling and leasing back, produce the incremental cash flow shown in Table 9.7. The incremental IRR is the effective cost of the capital raised by the sale and leaseback, arising from the future need to pay rent and from the loss of capital growth in the property sold.

Therefore, the *direct* costs of the three sources of capital are as follows:

Bond issue = 5.0%;
Sale and leaseback = 9.7%;
Equity issue = 10.8%.

All-important to the decision is the impact on the company's gearing. The company should aim for a financial structure as close to the optimal as possible, but the question does not provide information to identify the gearing ratio that would result from raising capital from each of the three sources.

If, as a result of the bond issue, the gearing outcome was optimal, then that would be the recommended solution, because debt capital is cheapest. However, the current gearing ratio of 30% seems high, even for a food retailer, and a further £50m of debt could take it well above the optimal. In that case, Fresco should decide between the sale and leaseback and the equity issue.

Sale and leaseback finance has the tax advantage of debt capital (rent is deductible) without the disadvantage of raising financial gearing. In fact, if capital raised by sale and leaseback is used to repay debt, it will reduce financial gearing. However, as rent is a prior charge, a sale and leaseback deal will increase the company's operational gearing. From a balance sheet perspective, the sale and leaseback looks attractive, but in reality it may increase the company's risk.

The preferred option in this case requires further information – not only about financial structure, but also about operational issues, such as Fresco's need to retain full control of its premises as owner-occupier.

Table 9.7 Example 9.3: incremental cash flow (£m)

	Years				
	0	*1–5*	*6–10*	*11–15*	*15*
Sale and leaseback	+49.250	–2.240	–2.928	–3.826	–
Retain property	–	–	–	–	+111.624
Incremental cash flow	+49.250	–2.240	–2.928	–3.826	–111.624

Incremental IRR = 9.7% per annum (by calculator).

SUMMARY

This chapter has examined the application of DCF techniques to assist the business occupier of property to make the decision whether to buy or lease property or, if an owner-occupier, whether to raise capital by sale and leaseback. In previous applications, we have stressed that DCF analysis is a tool to assist decision-making, and not a substitute for judgement. That is particularly true in the applications examined in this chapter. In any particular case, there may be many financial and operational issues relevant to the decision that cannot be reflected and quantified accurately in a DCF analysis.

SELF-ASSESSMENT QUESTION

9.1 Polyprop Products plc, which manufactures components for the construction industry, will shortly be moving to new and larger accommodation because of business expansion. The new premises are being developed to Polyprop's specification in a new, well-located industrial estate. The company has provisionally agreed terms with the developer for either buying or leasing the new premises, and now needs to decide between the options.

Buy option
Agreed price: £2m (attributable to land £0.2m, building £1.6m, plant and machinery £0.2m).

Lease option
Agreed lease terms: rent £150,000 per annum, 15-year FRI lease subject to five-year reviews.

Polyprop is a well-run manufacturing company whose business qualifies for Industrial Buildings Allowances. It maintains a 25% gearing ratio (debt:total capital) and its equities and bonds yield 4% and 6½% respectively in the stock market. Its stockbrokers have recently predicted dividend growth averaging 5% per annum into the foreseeable future. If Polyprop elects to buy the property, the purchase will be financed out of the company's liquid capital reserves.

Advise Polyprop whether to buy or lease its new property. Assume the following:

- A ten-year period of occupation;
- All cash flows occur annually in arrears;

- The expected rental growth rate for modern industrial property is 2% per annum;
- Under both options, Polyprop would buy the plant and machinery from the developer;
- The cost of building repairs and insurance would be identical under each option;
- Stamp duty on purchase is 4% of price, and legal fees 0.5%;
- Legal fees of £2,500 would be payable on taking up the lease option;
- Corporation tax is payable on profits at a rate of 30%, payable in the same year as profits are earned; and
- Polyprop makes sufficient profits from its business to benefit annually from tax allowances.

ANSWER TO SELF-ASSESSMENT QUESTION

9.1 *Buy option*

As plant and machinery would be owned by Polyprop under both options, all related cash flows should be omitted, including tax allowances.

Purchase cost:
1.8 (1 + 0.045) = £1.881m.

Annual industrial building allowance:
4% of £1,600,000 = £64,000
Annual value at 30% tax = £19,200

Notional sale price, Year 10:

Estimated rental value, Year 10: 150,000 $(1 + 0.02)^{10}$ =	£182,849
Years purchase in perpetuity, say, 10%	10
	£1,828,490

As the sale in Year 10 is notional only, no allowance has been made for sale costs or the probability of being required to repay the IBA benefit through a balancing charge.

Lease option:
Expected net rental payments:

Years 1–5: 150,000 (1 − 0.3) = £105,000; and
Years 6–10: 150,000 $(1 + 0.02)^5$ (1 − 0.3) = £115,928.

Calculation of Incremental IRR
The cash flows are detailed in Table 9.8.

Polyprop's cost of capital

Equity: 4.2 + 5.0 = 9.2%
Debt: 6.5 (1 – 0.3) = 4.55%
WACC = (0.75 x 9.2) + (0.25 x 4.55) = 8.0%.

The incremental IRR is 6.7% per annum. This is the effective return expected on the extra cost of the buy option, gained primarily through avoiding the payment of rent and from the benefit of the annual IBA (which is not available under the lease option). The incremental IRR is 1.3% below Polyprop's WACC, which *prima facie* might suggest a lease decision. However, Polyprop's target return on the cost of purchase should reflect the risk of the investment relative to that of the company. Investing in a property for owner-occupation seems low risk compared with the business of manufacturing products for the (cyclical) building industry. That could perhaps justify a 1.3% discount on the WACC, but we do not know enough about Polyprop to make a clear decision. The decision should depend on the judgement of directors with a detailed knowledge of Polyprop's finances and operations.

Table 9.8 Incremental cash flow, SAQ 9.1

Year	*Purchase/ Sale (£)*	*IBA value (£)*	*Buy option (£)*	*Lease option (£)*	*Incremental cash flow (£)*
0	–1,881,000		–1,881,000	–2,500	–1,878,500
1		+19,200	+19,200	–105,000	+124,200
2		+19,200	+19,200	–105,000	+124,200
3		+19,200	+19,200	–105,000	+124,200
4		+19,200	+19,200	–105,000	+124,200
5		+19,200	+19,200	–105,000	+124,200
6		+19,200	+19,200	–115,928	+135,128
7		+19,200	+19,200	–115,928	+135,128
8		+19,200	+19,200	–115,928	+135,128
9		+19,200	+19,200	–115,928	+135,128
10	+1,828,490	+19,200	+1,847,690	–115,928	+1,963,618

Incremental IRR = 6.7% per annum (by calculator)

10

Risk Analysis in Cash-flow Appraisal

OVERVIEW

The objective of this chapter is to introduce three methods of risk analysis commonly undertaken alongside a DCF appraisal and often integrated with software packages for computer-based appraisal. The most sophisticated method, Monte Carlo simulation, extends beyond the scope of this book and is outlined only briefly here. Sensitivity and Scenario analyses are applicable to the appraisal of both standing investments and development projects. They make up an important discipline to provide the decision-maker with an improved sense of the investment's risk.

RISK IN PROPERTY APPRAISAL

So far, in this book, it has been assumed that an investment's risk can be allowed for merely by adjusting the target return, on the assumption that the higher the risk, the higher the return investors require. Three methods of risk adjustment have been introduced:

- Adding a subjectively-assessed risk premium on to a risk-free (or low-risk) rate of return;
- Adding or subtracting a subjectively-assessed risk premium or discount to or from a corporate investor's WACC; and
- Using the CAPM to calculate the risk premium to add to a risk-free rate of return.

In view of such allowances, the reader might wonder whether there is a need for any further action to deal with risk. There is, for three main reasons. First, in each of the three methods above, the appraiser is required to make judgements about risk. This is true even when applying the CAPM, because of the difficulty in identifying the beta of an investment or project. Sound judgement requires a 'feel' for the investment's risk which requires, in turn, an investigation into the investment's potential to produce a different return from that expected; in particular, the potential for a nasty surprise.

Second, by revealing the level of risk and identifying its sources, risk analysis can highlight the need to control risk, and indicate ways in which it can be controlled or mitigated.

Third, calculation of a single best-estimate NPV or IRR does not provide a sufficient basis for selecting one risky investment in preference to another. If a project is risky, this means there will be a range of possible outcomes, above and below the NPV or IRR calculated in the appraisal. Two investments might have identical NPVs, but very different ranges of possible outcomes. Arguably, the NPV or IRR only reveals half the story, and the decision-maker needs further information about the investments' risks in order to make a rational choice between them. The purpose of risk analysis is to reveal the uncertainties that are obscured by using best-estimate figures ('point estimates') in cash flows. Reality is a range of possible values for each variable, and a range of possible outcomes for the investment.

Investment risk is a complex subject with many facets. In considering risk analysis in the context of DCF appraisal, the challenge is to identify and measure the risk that really matters to the investor. As an asset class, the risk of standing property (measured as the standard deviation of annual returns) is well below that of equity shares and similar to that of gilts. As an asset class, or even at the level of a large, well-diversified portfolio, the returns and risk of commercial property are determined primarily by the economy driving tenant demand, rental values and yields. But the performance of property also depends on the vagaries of the property market and its tendency to lurch into occasional boom/bust cycles. In addition, at the level of the individual property, further risk derives from the property's characteristics arising from its location, building and lease.

In so far as the performance of property investment is driven by the national economy, much of the risk will be market-related rather than specific risk. It must also vary over time. Sometimes risk will be low, sometimes it will be high; for example, at the peak of a cycle. Therefore, risk analysis should take into account the economic context and involve forecasting. The techniques of risk analysis are of limited value without forecasts.

The risk of property development is normally much greater than the risk of investing in an equivalent standing property. Major property companies have been brought down by failed development projects. Primarily, the extra risk arises because a development's returns are a volatile residual; the difference between the value at completion and the development's costs. Therefore, the variables that determine development risk are those that determine the risk of standing property (primarily rent voids and fluctuating rental values and yields), together with construction and finance costs.

The source and nature of risk also varies with the investment's time-scale. The risk of a two-year development project must tend to be greater than that of a one-year project, because of the extra scope for the crucial variables to move in response to economic change. In the case of standing investments, the relative importance of rental value and yield change will depend on the time-scale. In the short term, yield fluctuations can be more important than rental change, but in the long run rental value fluctuations will usually be more significant.

In seeking to identify and analyse the risk that should concern the investor, it is important to remember two conclusions from Chapter 7:

(i) What matters is the risk that an investment brings to the investor's portfolio, not the investment's risk in isolation;
(ii) The risk perspective of a company should be distinguished from that of an institution.

The prime responsibility of a company is to maximise shareholder value. Shareholders can easily avoid specific risk by diversifying their portfolios of equities. They do not need companies to do the diversification on their behalf, and there is no double gain from diversification by both parties. Therefore, the corporate investor should not strive to reduce specific risk at the cost of lower returns (except, perhaps, by avoiding large, risky projects that might put the company in peril). Nor should a company seek to minimise market-related risk. The objective should be high return *relative* to market risk. This suggests a policy of focus; for example, specialisation in some particular property type, sector or location. Highest returns will tend to be earned by companies with the greatest expertise or other comparative advantage.

By contrast, life or pension funds cannot assume that their beneficiaries hold diversified investment portfolios. Therefore, they should seek to diversify out of specific risk. But research suggests (Brown and Matysiak, 2000) that it is much more difficult to diversify away the specific risk in a property portfolio than in a share portfolio. It needs a lot of properties and a conscious policy of seeking out investments whose returns tend to show a low correlation with the existing portfolio.

The issues raised above are important, and provide useful concepts to assist the decision-maker in making judgements about selecting or rejecting investments. However, in reality, it is not practicable to distinguish clearly an investment's specific risk from its market-related risk, nor to distinguish its risk in the investor's portfolio from its risk in isolation. The practice of controlling risk falls well short of the theory.

A simple but useful definition of investment risk is the capacity of the actual return to vary from the expected return. Ideally, for any investment, the decision-maker would have a frequency distribution that defines the full range of possible NPV or IRR outcomes and the probability of each. Two such distributions are shown in Figure 10.1. These are both 'normal' distributions – that is, where returns are distributed symmetrically above and below the mean. The mean (or Expected) return is identical for both investments ($\bar{r}$), but the risk is much greater for B, as shown by its wider dispersion of possible returns above and below the mean (measured by the standard deviation, σ). If the investments could be repeated an infinite number of times, the mean would represent the average return. But most projects can only be undertaken once, so a probability distribution provides a view of the likelihood of any possible return, or of an acceptable (or unacceptable) return being achieved. If a choice had to be made between A or B, A would be preferred by all investors except those positively attracted by risk.

In the case of investments with a normal distribution, performance can be defined by the mean return and either the variance or standard deviation, which both measure the dispersion of possible returns around the mean. But the distribution of returns may be asymmetrical or skewed (see Figure 10.2). If returns are positively skewed, most of the risk is 'up-side', but if negatively skewed, most of the risk is 'down-side'; that is, there is a long 'tail' of possible low or negative returns.

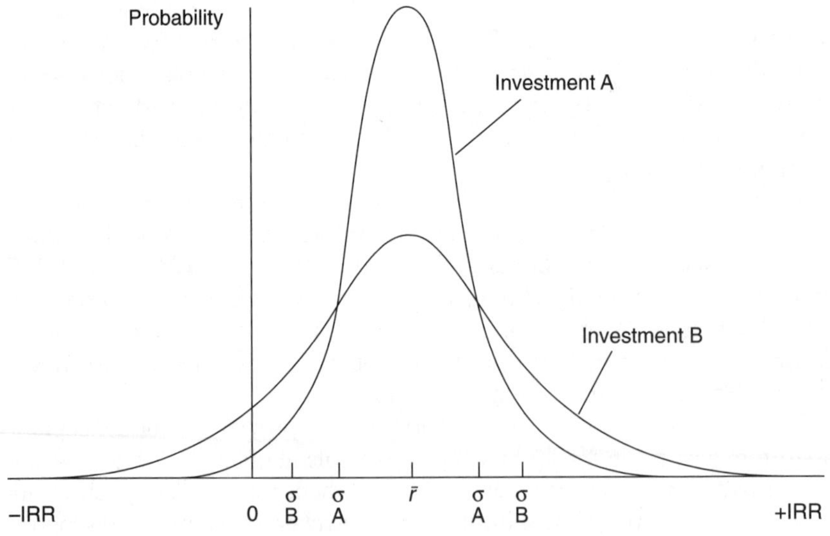

Figure 10.1 *Normal distributions: investments A and B*

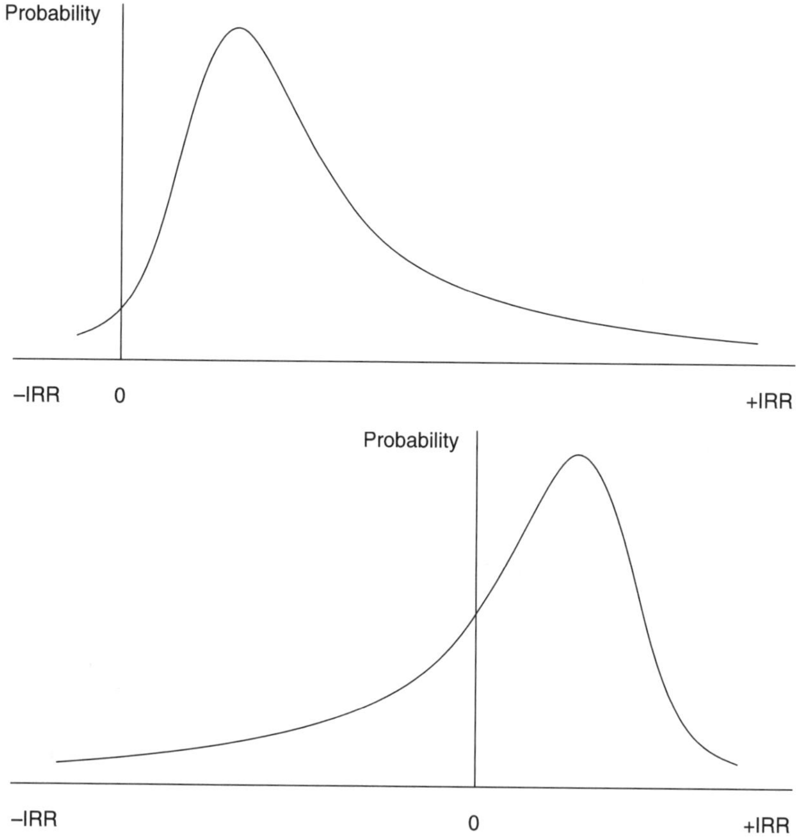

Figure 10.2 *Skewed distributions*

MONTE CARLO SIMULATION

In order to create a probability distribution for a project which can only be undertaken once, a process of simulation is employed. The preferred technique is called Monte Carlo simulation (because the selection of random numbers for each variable input is comparable to that of a roulette wheel). The variability of a project's return depends on the variability of its inputs; for example, in the case of a development project, building cost, project duration, rental value, yield on completion and so on. Therefore, the process involves identifying these variable factors, defining their probability distributions and inter-relationships, and calculating the NPV or IRR outcome many times using sample values for each variable, repeated according to their probabilities. Such a process is easily handled by computer, and the output is a probability distribution of the range of possible NPV or IRR outcomes for the project. This provides the decision-maker with all accessible information on the project's risk and return, in statistical or graphical form.

The accuracy of a Monte Carlo simulation necessarily depends on the accuracy of the input data. As the Americans say, 'garbage in, garbage out'. It is scepticism about the ability to specify realistic ranges and probabilities for the input variables, together with lack of familiarity and trust in the technique, which probably explains why it is not used more frequently. It seems particularly suited to the appraisal of property development, where risk is greater and more complex than for standing investments. But detailed development appraisal is beyond the scope of this book, and the technique is not examined further here. However, the reader is referred to Byrne (1996), for a full description of its application to the appraisal of property development.

SENSITIVITY ANALYSIS

The purpose of sensitivity analysis is to identify the main sources of an investment's risk, and their relative importance, with a view to taking action to control or mitigate the risk. Risk arises from fluctuations in the variable factors that determine returns, and sensitivity analysis essentially involves examining the impact on returns (NPV or IRR) resulting from a change in each of these variable factors, while the other variables are held constant at their expected values. Standard approaches include:

- measuring the effect on NPV or IRR of, say, a 10% change above and below the expected value of each factor, to see which factors have the greatest effect on the investment's return; and
- measuring what percentage change in each factor would result in the investment just breaking even (where NPV = 0).

However, a major weakness of these basic forms of sensitivity analysis is that they assume that each variable is equally volatile. This is unlikely. Analysis might show that a project is vulnerable to a 10% adverse swing in either rents or building cost but the probability of rents moving by 10% may be very different from that of the building cost. Nor are variables necessarily equally volatile above and below their expected values. The analysis needs to take into account the differing volatility of the variables, not in general, but specifically over the period of the proposed investment or project.

An improved version of the technique (Hirst, 2001) is to identify upper and lower limits to the potential fluctuation of each variable, and to test the impact of movements within these parameters. These limits or 'bounds' should be defined, not as absolute limits (which would tend to be infinite), but values that have a 90% probability of not being exceeded. In other words, for any factor there would be a 10% chance of the value coming below the lower bound, and a 10% chance of it exceeding the higher bound. Bounds would be identified by consultation with relevant experts; for example, a quantity surveyor in the case of building cost, and a letting agent in the case of rents. In some cases, upper and lower values may be little better than guesstimates but, overall, the process should introduce greater realism into the analysis.

The analysis will be illustrated by means of a simplified example of a property refurbishment that is to be completed and sold within a year.

Example 10.1

Criterion Estates owns a vacant property, recently valued at £4m, which it plans to refurbish and sell in 12 months' time. The cost of building work and related fees has been estimated at £5m, and the sale price is expected to be £10m, comprising a rent of £700,000 and a rental yield of 7%.

After negotiations with potential tenants and investors, Criterion has provisional agreements to pre-let and pre-sell the completed project, but at the rent and yield prevailing in the market at the date of completion. Hence, three variable factors will determine the project's profitability, namely building cost, rental value and yield at completion. The value of the existing property is a constant. Assume all payments and the sale proceeds occur at the year end, and that Criterion's target return is 15%. Tax and selling costs are ignored.

We shall undertake two sensitivity analyses here in order to illustrate points made earlier. The first is a traditional but naïve analysis which ignores the relative volatility of the three variables and the economic context. The second takes into account the context and is based on bounds for the three variables.

Naïve Analysis

In view of the simplifying assumptions that the project has a one-year duration, and that all income and expenditure is at the year end, the project's expected IRR is simply the expected £1m surplus as a percentage of the Year 0 opportunity cost of £4m – that is, 25% IRR, represented as follows:

$$\text{IRR} = \frac{\left[\left(\frac{100}{a} \times b\right) - c\right] - 4.0}{4.0} \qquad (10.1)$$

where a = yield at completion;
b = rental value at completion; and
c = building cost.

Therefore, the expected IRR is:

$$\frac{\left[\left(\frac{100}{7} \times 0.7\right) - 5.0\right] - 4.0}{4.0} = 25\%$$

It is a simple matter to find the value for each variable that would result in the project just breaking even; that is, where IRR = 15% and NPV = 0. In more realistic examples, trial and error would be required, although these values can be found by using a spreadsheet on a computer.

(1) Find the property's *yield* at completion which would result in an IRR of 15% while other variables remain constant:

$$0.15 = \frac{\left[\left(\frac{100}{a} \times 0.7\right) - 5.0\right] - 4.0}{4.0}$$

a = 7.292%

So, a 4.2% rise in the market yield (from 7%) would result in the project just breaking even.

(2) Find the *rental value* at completion which would result in the IRR = 15%

$$0.15 = \frac{\left[\left(\frac{100}{7} \times b\right) - 5.0\right] - 4.0}{4.0}$$

b = £672,000

So, a 4.0% fall in the rent (from £700,000) would result in the project just breaking even.

(3) Find the *building cost* which would result in the IRR = 15%:

$$0.15 = \frac{\left[\left(\frac{100}{7} \times 0.7\right) - c\right] - 4.0}{4.0}$$

c = £5.4m

So, an 8.0% rise in the building cost (from £5m) would result in the project just breaking even.

The conclusion of this analysis is that the project is sensitive to small adverse changes in the property's yield and rental value, but less sensitive to a rise in building costs.

Realistic Analysis in Market Context

As explained, the analysis above abstracts from the economic and market context, and ignores the relative likelihood of adverse changes in each of the variables in that context. We shall now assume that the economy and the property market are both on an improving trend. The risk from a change of yield is thought to be mainly on the up-side; that is, more likely to move beneficially than adversely. On the other hand, construction costs are tending to rise because of strengthening demand; in that case, the risk is considered to be mainly down-side.

It is assumed that Criterion Estates has now consulted the relevant experts, resulting in the following bounds for the three variables:

	Lower bound	*Upper bound*
Yield	6.5%	7.25%
Rental value	£650,000	£750,000
Building cost	£4.5m	£6m

Using Equation (10.1), we calculate the IRR outcomes that would result from the value of each factor varying within these bounds. These are shown in Table 10.1 and Figure 10.3 (represented by the diagonal lines).

In contrast to the first analysis, which showed yield and rental value as the most sensitive variables, this more realistic analysis reveals building cost

Table 10.1 Sensitivity analysis, Criterion Estates

Yield (%)	*IRR (%)*	*Rental value (£)*	*IRR (%)*	*Building cost (£m)*	*IRR (%) (£)*
6.50	44.2	650,000	7.1		
6.75	34.3	675,000	16.1	4.5	37.5
7.00	25.0	700,000	25.0	5.0	25.0
7.25	16.4	725,000	33.9	5.5	12.5
		750,000	42.9	6.0	Nil

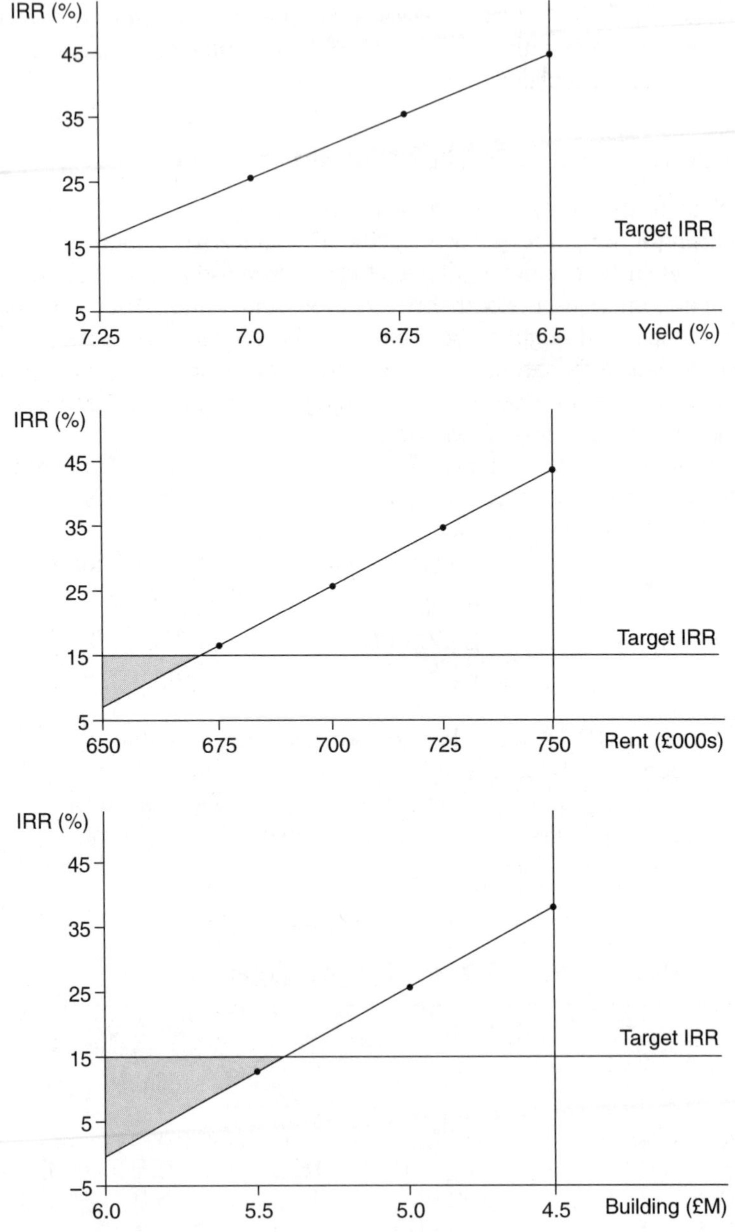

Figure 10.3 *Sensitivity analysis, Criterion Estates*

to be the most important factor requiring attention. This is illustrated by the size of the shaded triangles in Figure 10.3, which identify the values for building cost and rent that result in a negative NPV (target IRR > IRR outcome). The yield variable produces no 'danger triangle'.

The purpose of sensitivity analysis is to identify the principal sources of risk with a view to taking action to control the risk. Having highlighted building cost as the main source of risk in this case, it would be logical to seek to reduce or control that cost; for example, by means of a fixed-price contract.

If the project was being proposed in a weakening economy, the most sensitive variable might be the rental value. In such a situation, it might be sensible not to proceed without a pre-let at an agreed rent. By such means, the developer would pass on the risk to the tenant. But the likelihood is that the outcome would be a reduction in the developer's return, as the rent that the tenant would agree to pay on a pre-let would tend to reflect the extra risk taken on.

SCENARIOS AND THE EXPECTED NPV

Sensitivity analysis tells the appraiser something about the *sources* of an investment's risk, and their relative importance. However, it says little about the investment's risk as a whole. In fact, it could be misleading, because the principal factors that determine returns tend not to vary independently but to move together either beneficially or adversely according to economic conditions. For example, in a typical post-war economic cycle, it was quite possible to have had rental values falling, rent voids increasing, and yields, finance costs and even construction costs all rising simultaneously in an economic downturn. Conversely, all or most of these critical variables could move to raise development profits in an economic upturn. Investors' returns from both standing property and development projects are driven by the economy.

This inter-relationship of the principal variables is taken into account in the Scenario approach to appraisal, which examines the impact on returns of different economic or market conditions ('states of nature'). It is usual to imagine three typical scenarios:

- A 'pessimistic' scenario – featuring, say, a down-turn in the economy;
- A 'most likely' scenario – featuring, say, stable economic conditions; and
- An 'optimistic' scenario – featuring, say, an up-turn in the economy.

For each scenario, values for each of the investment's variables are selected (in conjunction with experts' advice) to be consistent with the conditions assumed, and the NPVs or IRRs calculated. These would provide the decision-maker with an indication of the variability of possible outcomes, although by no means the full range that would result from more extreme conditions. In effect, each scenario is representing a wider range of possible values, above and below those used in calculating the NPV or IRR.

The analysis can be extended by allocating probabilities to each of the scenarios (summing to 1.0), and calculating the investment's Expected NPV by summing the product of the NPV and the probability for each of these scenarios. The Expected NPV (or Expected IRR) is a weighted average NPV (or IRR). The term 'Expected' here represents the arithmetic mean, a rather different meaning than 'expected IRR' used previously in this book. The method is best illustrated by an example.

Example 10.2

Orion Properties is appraising a development project which it expects to be completed in two years' time. The cost of construction and related fees are expected to amount to £12m, and the value at completion to be £20m, comprising a rent of £1.2m and a yield of 6%. Orion already owns the site which has recently been valued at £5m. In order to simplify the example, we shall again assume that the property has been pre-let and pre-sold at the rental value and yield prevailing at the date of completion. There are therefore three principal variables determining the developer's return; namely, rental value, yield and construction cost. It is also assumed that one third of the construction costs will be paid in Year 1, and two thirds in Year 2, and that all cash flows occur at the year end. Orion's target return is 15%. Tax is ignored.

The values for each of the variables under three economic scenarios (most likely, optimistic and pessimistic scenarios) have been agreed by Orion in discussions with their consultants, and are shown in Table 10.2, along with the NPV and IRR outcome under each scenario and the probability of each scenario. The Expected NPV and Expected IRR are calculated as follows:

$$\text{Expected (mean) NPV} = (0.2 \times 3.821) + (0.6 \times 0.595) + (0.2 \times -3.598)$$
$$= +£0.401$$
$$\text{Expected (mean) IRR} = (0.2 \times 45.1) + (0.6 \times 20.0) + (0.2 \times -18.4)$$
$$= 17.34\%$$

As the Expected NPV is positive and the Expected IRR exceeds the target IRR, this project should be accepted, *unless* the risks exposed by the pessimistic scenario convince Orion that their target IRR of 15% is too low and should be raised above 17.34%! Note that the Expected NPV and Expected IRR are both below the NPV and IRR in the most likely scenario.

Table 10.2 Scenario analysis, Orion Properties

	Scenario		
	Optimistic	*Most likely*	*Pessimistic*
Probability	0.2	0.6	0.2
Construction cost	£11.4m	£12.0m	£13.2m
Rental value	£1.3m	£1.2m	£1.1m
Yield	5.5%	6.0%	7.0%
IRR per annum	45.1%	20.0%	–18.4%
NPV @ 15% per annum	+£3.821m	+£0.595m	–£3.598

This is because the rise in the property's yield and the construction cost assumed under the pessimistic scenario is greater than the reduction assumed under the optimistic scenario. Returns are negatively skewed.

Although the assumptions made in this example over-simplify the complexities of a development project, the pessimistic scenario has demonstrated well the high risks to which property developers are exposed (and the optimistic scenario demonstrates the large profit that can be earned) because of changing economic and market conditions. Scenario analysis provides an insight into project risk, and the Expected NPV (like an NPV calculated using a risk-adjusted discount rate) has introduced an allowance for risk, but it has not really measured risk. If, however, an assumption is made that the range of possible outcomes from a project has the characteristics of a normal distribution, then it is possible to use scenarios to calculate the probability of the project failing to earn a positive NPV (by reference to the area under a normal curve (see Byrne, 1996, or Lumby, 1998). None the less, depending on the accuracy with which values and probabilities can be ascribed to the variables, a Monte Carlo analysis should be more reliable.

Sensitivity, Scenario and Monte Carlo techniques are incorporated into various software packages available for computer-based appraisal. These model the development process and help to avoid much of the drudgery and complexity otherwise entailed.

APPRAISAL IN EQUITY ANALYSIS

It is always interesting and potentially useful for the property adviser to keep an eye on practices employed for appraising other investments, particularly equity shares. One might expect that lessons in risk analysis could be learned from techniques used by analysts of risky equities such as electronics or biotech stocks (although cash flows from property investments and projects are highly predictable by comparison).

In the case of young companies that have yet to become profitable but whose prospects are bright, appraisal methods range from the use of simple units of comparison to the application of real option pricing models (a technique also explored by property analysts). However, DCF is probably the standard technique, typically by estimating cash flows over a ten-year period followed by a terminal value. The discount rate applied is normally a risk-adjusted WACC, after estimating the company's cost of equity by reference to the CAPM.

The overwhelming emphasis in appraisal is placed on predicting cash flows. Risk appraisal might include some sensitivity analysis; for example, to test the impact on the share valuation of changed assumptions about the growth rate adopted. Probabilities are used in the appraisal of pharmaceutical or biotech stocks to value prospective drugs in the development pipeline. Based on historic evidence, the probabilities of a drug eventually reaching the marketplace typically range from 0.08 to 0.90, depending on the stage reached in clinical tests.

Otherwise, little risk analysis is normally undertaken. It seems that the equity investor relies largely on portfolio diversification and balance to take care of risk. It might be said that the widespread over-valuation of technology stocks in the late 1990s could be explained, in part, by the lack of sophisticated analysis. But sophistication does not ensure accuracy. More likely, it would have made little difference. The excessive optimism of both the market and analysts would have still prevailed. For the future, in both equity and property appraisal, it is better to concentrate on being 'roughly right' than to get it 'precisely wrong'.

SUMMARY

This chapter has introduced three techniques for assessing the risk of property investments or developments that can be used alongside a conventional DCF appraisal. The most sophisticated of these is Monte Carlo simulation, which is mainly applicable to development projects, and provides a detailed statistical map of a project's risk. It is the ideal, provided there is confidence in the values and probabilities ascribed to the variable factors. Sensitivity analysis and scenarios, which are applicable to the appraisal of both developments and standing property, have more modest objectives. The main function of sensitivity analysis is to identify the principal sources of risk with a view to taking action to control that risk, whereas scenarios provide an indication of how the investment's returns can vary according to changing economic and market conditions. In all cases, the analysis should help the decision-maker to gain a feel for the investment's risk and assist in arriving at a judgement.

SELF-ASSESSMENT QUESTIONS

10.1 A tax-exempt investor is considering a long-term investment in a high-quality freehold retail property recently let at a rent of £60,000 per annum FRI, on a long lease subject to five year rent reviews. The price is £1m. The investor's target return is 8.5% per annum and average rental growth of 4% per annum is expected into the foreseeable future. Assume rent is paid annually in arrears.

(a) What would be the impact on the IRR if rental growth only averages 3.5% per annum?
(b) What lower rate of rental growth would make the investment unjustifiable?

10.2 Albion Properties is appraising a development project with a view to making a decision on whether to proceed. It has an option to buy the site at an agreed price, and has made a provisional agreement to pre-let the completed property. Albion intends to sell the property at the project's completion, but is concerned about the possible impact on profitability of a change in rental yield and construction cost. The values for both of these variables under three economic scenarios, as well as the probability of each scenario, have been agreed with Albion's consultants and are shown below, together with the NPV outcome of each scenario using a risk-adjusted target return of 17%. Taxation has been ignored. Calculate the project's Expected NPV and advise Albion whether to proceed or not.

	Scenario		
	Optimistic	*Most likely*	*Pessimistic*
Probability	0.25	0.50	0.25
Construction costs, etc.	£700,000	£750,000	£850,000
Yield at completion	6.50%	7.00%	7.75%
NPV @ 17%	£216,634	£79,975	–£123,655

ANSWERS TO SELF-ASSESSMENT QUESTIONS

10.1 This is a simple application of sensitivity analysis to a standing investment. For the long-term investor, rental growth is the most important variable, and it is important to consider the effect of growth failing to match expectations.

As the property is let at its rental value, the lease is long, the next review and subsequent reviews are at five-year intervals, and rent is paid annually in arrears, we can use short-cut DCF techniques.

(a) The expected IRR on the assumption of 3.5% growth is the IRR of the following cash flow:

Expected cash flow (£m)

	Years	
0	1–5	5
–1.0	+0.06	$+1.0\ (1 + 0.035)^5$

Expected IRR = 9.13% per annum (by calculator). Similarly, the expected IRR on the assumption of 4% rental growth is 9.58% per annum. Therefore, the effect of the reduced growth would be to reduce the IRR by 0.45% per annum.

(b) Calculate the rental value growth rate which would result in a nil NPV (expected IRR = target IRR):

$$g = \left[\frac{(r - y)(1 + r)^n + y}{r}\right]^{1/n} - 1$$

$$= \left[\frac{(0.085 - 0.06)(1 + 0.085)^5 + 0.06}{0.085}\right]^{1/5} - 1$$

$= 0.0280$
$= 2.80\%$ per annum

2.80% is the rental growth rate required to provide an IRR of 8.5% per annum. Therefore, any growth rate averaging less than 2.8% would make the investment unjustifiable.

10.2 ENPV = (0.25 × £216,634) + (0.50 × £79,975) + (0.25 × –£123,655)
= £63,232.

The ENPV is positive, so the project should proceed provided that Albion is able to sustain the potential loss of the pessimistic outcome.

Bibliography

Arnold, G. (2002) *Corporate Financial Management*, 2nd edn (Harlow: Financial Times/Prentice-Hall).

Barclays Capital (2000) *Equity–Gilt Study 2000* (London: Barclays Capital).

Baum, A. and Crosby, N. (1995) *Property Investment Appraisal,* 2nd edn (London: Thomson).

Bowcock, P. and Bayfield, N. (2000) *Excel for Surveyors* (London: Estates Gazette).

Brayshaw, R. E. (1992) *The Concise Guide to Company Finance and its Management* (London: Chapman & Hall).

Brealey, R. A. and Myers, S. C. (2002) *Principles of Corporate Finance*, 7th edn (New York: McGraw Hill).

Brown, G. R. and Matysiak, G. A. (2000) *Real Estate Investment* (Harlow: Financial Times/Prentice Hall).

Byrne, P. (1996), *Risk, Uncertainty and Decision-Making in Property Development,* 2nd edn (London: E. & F.N. Spon).

Cohen, N. (1998) 'Chanting the mantra of cheap capital', *Financial Times*, 4 September.

Davidson, A. W. (2002) *Parry's Valuation and Investment Tables*, 12th edn, (London: Estates Gazette).

DTZ Debenham Thorpe (1997) *Money into Property* (London: DTZ Debenham Thorpe).

Fraser, W. D. (1986), 'Property yield trends in a fluctuating economy', *Journal of Valuation*, vol. 4, no. 3.

Hirst, I. (2001) *Investment Appraisal for Shareholder Value* (Harlow: Financial Times/Prentice Hall).

Homer, A. and Burrows, R. (2002) *Tolley's Tax Guide (*Butterworth Tolley).

IPD (2003) *IPD UK Annual Index* (London: Investment Property Databank).

Isaac, D. (1998) *Property Investment* (London: Macmillan).

Keynes, J. M. (1931) 'Economic possibilities for our grandchildren' in *Essays in Persuasion* (London: Macmillan).

Leishman, C. (2003) *Real Estate Market Research and Analysis* (Basingstoke: Palgrave).

London Business School, *Risk Measurement Service,* L.B.S. Financial Services Quarterly.

Lumby, S. (1998), *Investment Appraisal and Financing Decisions*, 6th edn (London: Chapman & Hall).

Rudd, R. (1994) 'Hanson increases investment payback time', *Financial Times*, 16 May.

Saigol, L. (2002) 'Six Ccontinents under fire from Hermes', *Financial Times*, 21 January.

Index

accounting profit, 12, 68
Adjusted Present Value (APV) method, 120–4, 125, 127, 128–30
annual equivalent rate (AER), 20
annualised rates, 20–1, 23–4
average return method, 9–12, 22–4, 48–9

benefit/cost ratio, 60–3, 70, 72
beta coefficient, 115–20, 124, 126, 128–9, 158
borrowing capacity, 121–4, 126, 129
buildings
  depreciation of, 78, 79–80, 81, 83–4, 93–9, 136–8, 140, 142
  repairs and insurance, 85–6, 95, 98–9,147–9, 152
buy or lease decisions, 143–50, 154–6

capital allowances, 81–4, 87, 90–1, 94–100, 144–5, 147, 150, 151–2
Capital Asset Pricing Model (CAPM), 104, 106, 114–21, 124–5, 129, 157, 170
capital gains tax, 78, 148
capital rationing, 60–3
certainty equivalents, 64
compounding, introduction to, 1–2, 14–18
computer-based appraisal, 157
corporation tax, 80–91, 94–100, 107–8, 110–11, 116, 118–19, 121–3, 127–9, 136, 144–53, 155–6
cost of capital, 47–9, 54, 59, 66, 71, 101–2, 104–17, 125–30, 136, 144
  of debt capital, 64–5, 104, 107–13, 125, 127–8, 152,
  of equity capital, 101, 104–17, 125, 127–8, 151
  opportunity cost of capital, 13, 66–7, 102, 111, 133
  weighted average cost of capital (WACC), 104, 110–14, 117, 120–1, 123–5, 128, 147, 149–50, 156, 157, 170
cum. div., 127

debt capacity, *see* borrowing capacity
depreciation, 78, 79–80, 81, 93–6, 103, 131, 136, 137–40, 142,148, 152
Descartes, 43
discounting, introduction to, 14–19, 23–6
disposal costs, 78
duration, 45, 58, 102, 161

Economic Value Added (EVA), 69
efficient markets, 105, 136
enterprise, 102, 104
equity earnings, 68
equity shares, 2–3, 7, 133, 158, 169–70
ex. div., 127
exit value, *see* terminal value
extended IRR method, 45, 52, 57

forecasting, 78, 158
frequency distribution, 160–2
future value, 14–18, 23–4

gearing, 3–7, 65, 117–19 153
  capital, 6
  financial, 5–7, 117, 150, 153
  income, 3–5, 6
  operational, 5, 110–11, 117, 120, 150, 153
  optimal or target, 104, 108–11, 121, 125, 153
gilts (UK government bonds), 2, 102–3, 105, 116, 124–6, 128, 133, 136, 158

growth, allowing for, 77–9, 88–90, 95, 97, 99, 131–42, 152

Hanson Trust, 68
Hermes, 68,
Holiday Inn, 68
hurdle rate, 101
 see also required return

Industrial Buildings Allowance (IBA), 81, 83–4, 94, 96–9, 147, 154–6
inflation, 2, 13, 102–3, 150
 allowing for, 77–9, 87, 89–90, 95, 98, 99
Intercontinental Hotels, 68
internal rate of return (IRR), 6, 32–40, 41–3, 51–8
 extended IRR, 45, 52, 57
 incremental IRR, 46–7, 53, 58, 144–6, 149, 153, 156
 IRR method and risk, 47, 49, 52–3
 relative merits, 48–50
 required IRR (determinants of),13–14, 63–4, 75–6, 101–20, 121, 124–6, 128–9, 149, 150
interpolation, 33–7

Keynes, John Maynard, 1

leaseback decisions, 150–4
leverage, *see* gearing
life assurance, 1, 2, 67, 102, 133, 159
liquidity, 13, 102–3, 133

machinery, *see* plant and machinery
market risk, 115, 124, 158–9
 see also beta coefficient
market's implied growth expectation (MIGE), 136–8, 141
MEPC, 68
Modern Portfolio Theory (MPT), 101, 115
Modigliani and Miller thesis, 109
Monte Carlo simulation, 157, 161–2, 169, 170
multiple positive roots (solutions), 43–5, 49, 52, 56–7
mutually exclusive projects, 45–7, 49, 62

negative capital outlay, 44, 56–7
net present value (NPV)
 introduction to, 27–30, 32, 37–40, 51, 55–6
 relative merits, 48–50
net terminal value (NTV)
 introduction to, 30–2, 37–40,
 relative merits, 48–50
normal distributions, 160

obsolescence, 78, 80, 97, 137–8, 152
opportunity cost, 13, 66–8, 73, 75, 102, 125
 of capital, 13, 67, 111, 133
overhead costs, 67

payback period, 9–12, 22–4, 48–9, 68
pension funds, 1, 3, 67, 83–4, 102, 133, 159
plant and machinery, 79–83, 91, 93–100, 144–5, 147, 151
portfolio theory, *see* Modern Portfolio Theory (MPT); Capital Asset Pricing Model (CAPM)
present value, 14–19, 23–6
probability distributions, *see* frequency distributions
project divisibility, 61
project independence, 61–3
property, performance of, 2–3, 158
property companies, 104, 118, 124

redemption yields, 102, 108, 124, 126, 133
reinvestment assumption, 43
rent-review period, 131–6, 139–40
required return, determination of, 13–14, 63–4, 75–6, 101–20, 121, 124–6, 128–9, 149, 150
rights issue, 106, 151
risk, 7, 47, 64–5, 101, 103, 118, 157–72
 market (or systematic) risk, 115, 120, 124
 premium, 13, 102–4, 106, 111–20, 124, 128, 157
 of property development, 120
 specific risk, 115, 124, 158–9

risk-adjusted discount rate (RADR), 13
risk-adjusted WACC, 111–14, 120–1, 123–5
  see also weighted average cost of capital
'roll-over' relief, 148, 151

sale and leaseback decisions, 150–4
scenario analysis, 157, 167–9, 170, 171–2
sensitivity analysis, 157, 162–7, 170, 171–2
short-cut DCF, 131–42
Six Continents plc, 68
skewed distributions, 160–1
specific risk, 115, 124, 158–9
stamp duty, 80, 92, 147, 155
standard deviation, 158, 160
sub-period rates, 19–21, 23–4, 74
sunk costs, 65–6, 68, 73, 92

target return, *see* required return
tax shelter (shield), 80, 122–3, 150
taxation, 59, 77, 79, 80–4, 103, 107, 150
  see also capital gains tax; corporation tax; stamp duty; VAT
terminal value, 7, 66, 75, 76, 78, 88, 92, 138, 170
time value of money, 11, 12–16, 17, 19, 21–2, 133
Treasury bills, 116

UK government bonds, *see* gilts

Value Added Tax (VAT), xii, 80

weighted average cost of capital (WACC), 104, 110–14, 117, 120–1, 123–5, 128, 147, 149–50, 156, 157, 170

yield premium, 102–3, 125, 128